THE 12

WEEK YEAR

FIELD GUIDE

THE 12 WEEK YEAR

FIELD GUIDE

BRIAN MORAN
MICHAEL LENNINGTON

WILEY

Library of Congress Cataloging-in-Publication Data

Names: Moran, Brian, 1959- author. | Lennington, Michael, 1958- author.
Title: The 12 week year field guide / Brian Moran, Michael Lennington.
Other titles: Twelve week year field guide
Description: Hoboken, New Jersey : John Wiley & Sons, Inc., 2018. |
  Identifiers: LCCN 2018027441 (print) | LCCN 2018029182 (ebook) | ISBN
  9781119475385 (Adobe PDF) | ISBN 9781119475378 (ePub) | ISBN 9781119475248
  (pbk.)
Subjects: LCSH: Success in business. | Success. | Organizational
  effectiveness.
Classification: LCC HF5386 (ebook) | LCC HF5386 .M7529 2018 (print) | DDC
  650.1–dc23
LC record available at https://lccn.loc.gov/2018027441

Printed in the United States of America

V10006937_121818

CONTENTS

PREFACE

WELCOME TO *The 12 Week Year Field Guide*!

In your hands is perhaps the most powerful approach to goal achievement you will ever encounter. It has been painstakingly developed over more than a decade of work with our clients, as we have helped to make them more successful.

Virtually everything we have learned about what it takes for you to be great is distilled into this unique 12 week system.

What we had to learn through years of trial-and-error effort is now presented here for you to apply immediately. In the info-packed pages that follow, we show you how to avoid the most common performance traps, and how to apply the time-proven practices of high performers.

This may be one of the highest returns on investment that you ever make in yourself. You will be challenged to step out and act on your vision. You will reorient your life around the fundamental principles and disciplines of success. Your results will multiply week after week.

You will know what you want to create in your life, and you will know how to create it. You will find yourself spending more and more time on the important things. You will reach your goals

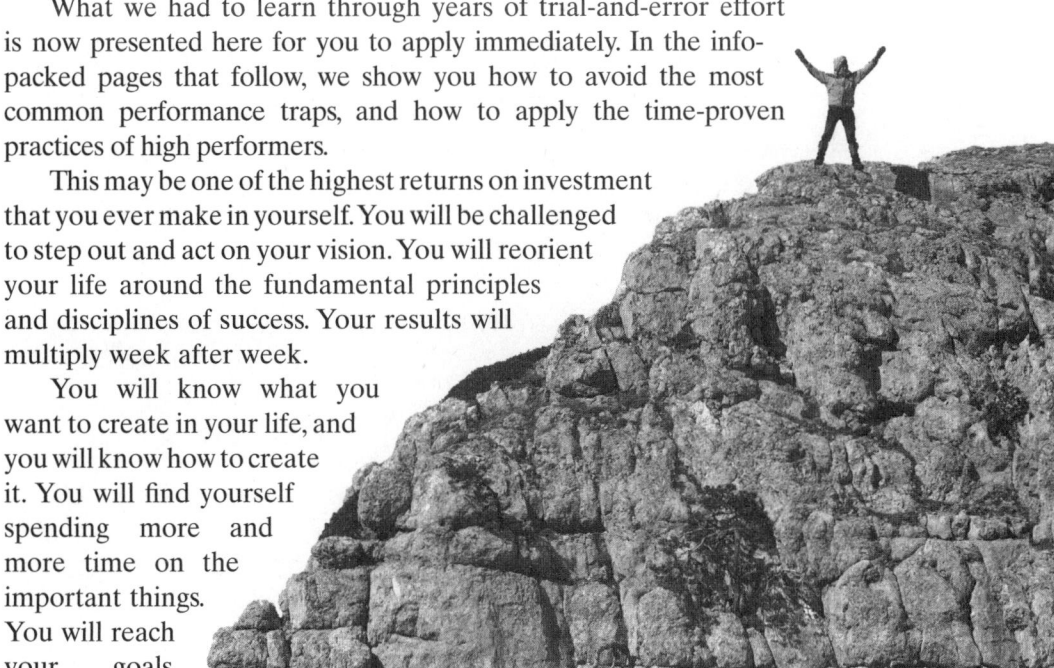

Credit: Olga Danylenko/Shutterstock.com.

faster than you ever thought possible. Simply put, the 12 Week Year, affectionately known as "12WY," will deliver your personal breakthrough.

Throughout this field guide, you will find a series of simple exercises designed to walk you through an easy-to-execute process of applying the concepts covered in the pages that follow. It is *strongly* recommended that you work on them in sequence and you are encouraged to begin each exercise when you are likely to have sufficient uninterrupted time to complete it.

Thank you for allowing us to be a part of your journey to personal and professional achievement. If you have questions along the way, feel free to email us at support@12weekyear.com.

We have also created some additional resources to accompany this field guide, to ensure that you get off to a strong start. Please visit www.12weekyear.com/fieldguide to access your free resources.

Here's to a great 12 weeks!

Be encouraged.

Brian Moran and Michael Lennington

Check us out on the Web!

www.12weekyear.com.

OVERVIEW OF THE 12 WEEK YEAR™

THIS FIELD GUIDE IS designed to support your application of the 12 Week Year (12WY) in any area of your life in which you seek improvement. It includes worksheets and tips designed to help you to effectively apply the principles and disciplines of the 12WY, and to accomplish your biggest goals faster.

While this guide is meant to stand alone, it is much more effective if you have read the *New York Times* bestselling book *The 12 Week Year* and have access to it as you work through this field guide.

Our book begins with a series of questions in Chapter 1:

1. How is it that some people seem to accomplish so much while the vast majority of people never accomplish what they are capable of?

2. If you could fully tap into your potential, what might be different for you?

3. How would your life change if each and every day you performed up to your full potential?

4. What would be different six months, three years, and five years down the road if each day you were at your best?"

You are starting a journey to discover *your* answers to these questions! Take a few minutes and imagine the accomplishments that you are capable of at your best. Capture them below:

- Physical - Strong, fit & healthy - optimal weight and an Ironman participant.
- Mental - focused, well read, committed & driven
- Emotional - happy, positive, high self-esteem loving, generous hearted, in the flow
- Business - Successful at what I put my focus on - publishing, wellness, teaching, wealth
- Family/home - Beautiful house, debt free, happy, healthy, successful kids

As you get started with this field guide, we hope that you have big expectations for yourself, and for the 12 Week Year. Big expectations are the important first step toward significant breakthrough. The more you expect, the greater your results with the 12 Week Year are likely to be.

Keep these expectations in mind as you work through the exercises in this field guide.

THE 12 WEEK YEAR

With roots in the proven athletic training discipline of Periodization, the 12 Week Year creates a concentrated focus on the key activities that drive results over short periods of time. Periodization is frequently used by world-class athletes, and now Brian Moran and Mike Lennington have adapted it for you to apply it both personally and professionally.

The 12 Week Year redefines your year. A year is now 12 weeks long, and with each new year, you get a fresh start!

Be aware that a 12 Week Year is very different from a "quarter." Quarterly planning and execution operate in the context of a 12 month year and foster the false belief that there is plenty of time to get things done, which results in less-than-optimal performance throughout the year.

This unproductive annualized thinking is eliminated with the 12 Week Year. Each 12 weeks stands on its own. 12 weeks *is* the year and in a 12 Week Year, the illusion of *lots of time* evaporates. The 12 Week Year narrows your focus to the week and to the day, which is where execution occurs.

For a deeper understanding of why a 12 Week Year drives better results than annual execution, see Chapter 2 in *The 12 Week Year*.

THE 12WY PRINCIPLES

The 12 Week Year is laid upon a foundation of three principles that ultimately determine an individual's effectiveness and success. These three principles are Accountability, Commitment, and Greatness in the Moment.

Let's take a closer look at each.

Accountability

Accountability is *ownership*. It is a character trait, a life stance, a willingness to own your actions and your results; regardless of the circumstances. The very nature of accountability rests on the understanding that each and every one of us has freedom of choice. It is this freedom of choice that is the foundation of personal accountability. The ultimate aim of

Accountability is to continually ask of ourselves, "What more can I do to get the result?" For more on Accountability, read Chapters 8 and 18 in *The 12 Week Year*.

Commitment

Commitment is a contract that you make with yourself to keep your promises. Keeping your promises to others builds strong relationships. Keeping promises with yourself builds integrity, self-esteem, and success.

Commitment and Accountability are closely related. In a sense, a commitment is your accountability projected into the future. It is your ownership of a future action or result.

Building a capacity for making and keeping commitments has a dramatic effect on your personal and business results. The 12 Week Year helps you to build the capacity to follow through on your critical commitments and achieve breakthrough in the important areas of your life. Chapters 9 and 19 of *The 12 Week Year* dig into the power of commitments and how to keep them effectively.

Greatness in the Moment

When do you become great? The obvious answer seems to be that you become great when you achieve your big goals, and are recognized by others. Yet greatness is not achieved when your results are reached. You become great long before your results show it. Greatness can happen in an instant; the moment you choose to do the things you need to do to be great, and each moment that you continue to choose to do those things. Results are not the essence of your greatness; your results are simply the confirmation of it.

Each and every one of us has the ability to be great. Being great is a discipline to do the things you know you need to do even when—*especially* when—you don't feel like it. For more on Greatness in the Moment, read Chapter 10 in *The 12 Week Year*.

These three principles—Accountability, Commitment, and Greatness in the Moment—form the foundation of personal and professional success.

———

THE 12WY DISCIPLINES

The 12 Week Year program addresses both the way you think (the three principles) and, in turn, the actions you take. At the action level, it concentrates on building capacity within a set of success disciplines that are required for effective execution. We have found that top performers—whether athletes or business professionals—are great not because their ideas are better, but because their *execution* disciplines are better.

Following the 12 Week Year will help you apply these disciplines in a way that leverages your current knowledge and fosters consistent action.

Vision—Vision fuels the 12 Week Year execution system. A compelling vision that aligns your personal and professional aspirations will help you take action even when you may not "feel" like it. Chapters 3 and 13 of the book provide more on how to leverage the power of Vision in your personal and professional life.

Planning—A 12 Week Plan starts with a 12 week goal that motivates you and aligns with your long-term vision. Each goal in your 12 Week Plan is supported by the tactics needed to reach it. When you craft your plan remember that "less is more." The more focused your plan is, the greater your chances of success. For more insight on planning well in the context of a 12 Week Year, read Chapters 4 and 14 of our book.

Process Control—Process Control consists of a set of tools and events that align your daily actions with the goals and tactics in your 12 Week Plan. Process Control ensures that you execute your tactics effectively. Chapters 5 and 15 of our book dig into the concepts and tools of Process Control.

Scorekeeping—Measurement drives your execution process. It is your anchor to reality. Effective measurement provides the comprehensive feedback necessary to stay on track and hit your goals. See Chapters 6 and 16 of the book for more on the power of Measurement.

Time Use—Everything that you accomplish happens in the context of the time you allocate to it. If you are not intentional with your time, then you are not in control of your results. Being intentional with your time is a must. The 12 Week Year itself is a different way of thinking about time—for more, read Chapters 7 and 17 of our book.

Every 12 weeks, you will build increased personal and team capacity by applying the three principles and five disciplines of the 12 Week Year (see Figure I.1).

One last note as you begin your journey with the 12 Week Year. There is always a gap between what you know and what you do. Sometimes the gap is small, sometimes it's huge. The issue is that there exists, for all of us, a knowing-doing gap.

This gap exists for the principles and disciplines of the 12 Week Year as well. People often intuitively "know" them. The problem arises when you think you know something, and you close yourself off from new learning in those areas. You rarely assess whether or not you are *actually applying* what you know as effectively as you can. Don't fall into that trap. Everyone can get better at each discipline and principle of the 12 Week Year even if they seem familiar.

Ensure that you leverage the elements of the 12 Week Year by engaging intensely and taking every opportunity to learn and improve.

THE 12 WEEK EXECUTION SYSTEM

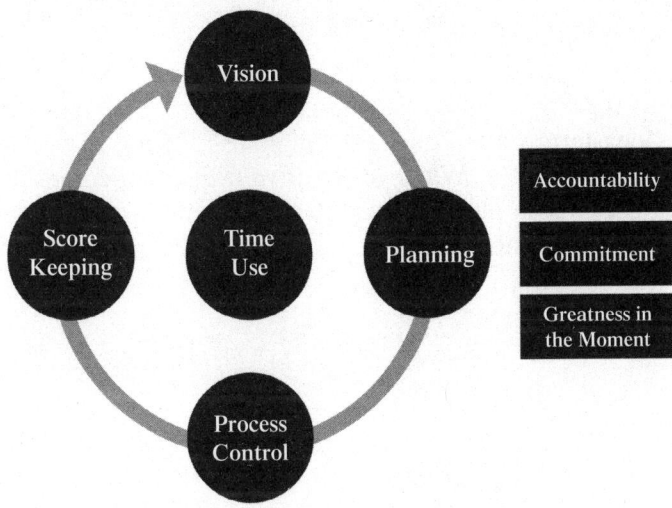

Figure I.1 The 12 Week Year is a closed system.

In Chapter 12 of our book, we talk about the 12 Week Year as a *closed system*. What we mean by that is that the 12 Week Year has everything that you need to take your goals, ideas, and drive to achieve great things.

Bring to it your big dreams and your breakthrough ideas, and it will help you to accomplish more in less time than ever before. Engage with each discipline and apply each principle—taken together they will help you to accomplish what you are capable of!

CHAPTER 1

Becoming a Visionary

The 12 Week Year journey begins with the first of the five disciplines—*Vision*. Your compelling vision provides the focus, direction, and energy needed for you to achieve extraordinary results. The best visions stretch you—they require your best work. Your "same-old, same-old" just won't do if you strive to become great at anything.

You will have to stretch yourself and when you stretch, you encounter resistance. Your old habits, thoughts, and systems will all push back at you.

Most change fails because the price required is too high. The ultimate price of change? Your comfort. That's why your vision is so important. It is your emotional and intellectual "why." It is the reason why you are willing to pay the price of change. If you have a vision that you are unwilling to abandon in the face of discomfort, you will become what you are capable of becoming.

The *first step* in creating your powerful vision is to imagine where you find yourself in 5, 10, 15, or even more years into the future. When you do this, something amazing happens. Neurons deep within your prefrontal cortex begin to fire. These neurons are the same ones that fire when you act on your vision. In a very real sense, when you imagine your future, you are training your brain to act on it as well.

SUCCESS TIP

Create a *big* vision. The larger your vision, the greater your results will be—big thinking always precedes big achievements. A big vision will call on you to deliver your very best. A big vision will give you permission to become more of what you are capable of.

On pages 79–81 of *The 12 Week Year*, we show how your thinking can often get in the way as you work on creating a big vision for yourself. If you have your copy of the book handy, take a look at these pages and learn what kinds of questions drive a big vision, and what kinds of questions get in the way. Then as you work through this chapter of the field guide, be aware of your thinking so that your vision is big enough to tap into what you are capable of in life.

In Exercise #1, which follows, you will do some initial vision work. While it may sound simple enough, vision work can require a fair amount of effort. In formulating your vision, let your mind stretch to imagine, and even embrace, the possibilities before you. These possibilities may be ones that you push aside in your daily life as being not immediate enough to command your attention, impractical, or even too audacious to even consider! There are no right or wrong answers in vision work. Please get comfortable, remove distractions, and let's get started.

───────

EXERCISE #1: HAVE—DO—BE

This first exercise is designed to "prime the pump" and to get you thinking about the possibilities for your life. Make it fun. Dream about the things that truly excite you.

Vision is the first place where you either expand, or limit, your results in life. Your goal is to create a stretch vision that is emotionally compelling for you, one that incorporates and strikes a balance between both your personal and professional aspirations.

As we begin, remember that you will have to push back against your limiting thinking. You may consider some big and challenging elements to your vision that will cause you to bump into what you believe are your current limits. You may even feel some fear or anxiety as you contemplate what it will take to reach your vision. Don't give in to that fear. It arises from your current thinking.

Anxiety creeps in when you begin to think that you don't know how to do something that is needed to reach your vision. That not knowing can make you feel uncomfortable. That discomfort can turn into anxiety and can ultimately even keep you from trying. Let go of your "How will I do this?" thoughts for a while! The question of "how" gets tackled in Chapter 2 of this field guide—the 12 Week Year Planning section.

For now, just focus on the question "What if?" What if you could accomplish your big vision? What would be different for you? For your family, friends, co-workers, team, community, family, place of worship, and so on.

To get started on your vision journey, you will work through an exercise called "Have—Do—Be." It will take about 20 minutes to complete, and it is a lot of fun!

Below is a table to capture your work. Start with the first column: "Have." Brainstorm all the things you would like to have in life, both material and nonmaterial. Perhaps you wish to have things like a cottage or second home, a great family, or financial security. Then stretch your thinking even further to include things that are well beyond your comfort zone—things like a private jet, or an island, or even a home in space!

In the end, some of the things will matter, make the final cut, and be part of your vision, and some won't. For now, just stretch. Work to fill the entire space provided.

Once the Have column is completed, repeat the same process with the Do and the Be columns. Ready? Let's get started.

DREAMS HOPES AND DESIRES

HAVE	DO	BE
A big georgian house	travel freely	healthy
A beautiful view	work that I love	happy
£10 million savings	- Pub/veatwel	content
Dog	wellness	financially wealthy
A campervan	- have lots of	success
healthy/strong body	time for exercise	energised
happy fulfilled life	I love - marathons	grateful
Very successful	- Ironman	strong
publishing business	- see friends	successful
Bestsellers in business	& family +	focused
fiction + childrens/	have lovely	committed
non fiction	ventures	mother
healthy/happy children	spend time	peaceful
holidays wherever I want	with children	social
Freedom to travel	Enjoy my life	
without restriction	every day	
Land with own	- spend time in	
watersource	my beautiful home	

Note that the output of the Have—Do—Be exercise *is not* your vison. It is simply a list of things that you want in your life; you are not committing to anything just yet. However, if some things show up in more than one column, they are likely to end up in your final vision. Keep this completed exercise handy—you will come back to it in the next exercise, your Long-Term Vision.

Natural swimming
pool
New interiences.

———

EXERCISE #2: LONG-TERM VISION

It's time to commit and to construct a vision of your life 5, 10, 15, or more years into the future. As you do this, pull from your Have—Do—Be lists. As other things occur to you as important, include them as well. Be bold, be courageous; create a life vision that inspires you and fulfills your purpose. There are no right or wrong answers. This is the life you deeply desire. Build your long-term vision below:

Long-Term Vision

In 5 years, I will be 57 years old. I will have ~~home~~ serenely retired having made enough money to be very comfortable for the rest of my blessed life. I have a very successful publishing and wellness business. The publishing company generates £750,000 per month passively. I now spend my time sharing helpful info to people who need the confidence to live an independent, wealthy (in all states) life. I have the most beautiful 8 bedroom home with spectacular views, a large sitting room + hallway that was made for christmas. I have made the house eco-friendly and I have my own natural water source. I love my natural swimming pool. I am the healthiest, sharpest + happiest I have been in my life + am deeply grateful for all the smallest clues that brought me here. The girls work hard + are happy + successful. I live a joyous, harmonious + blessed life which is wealthy on all levels

The next step is to craft your three-year vision—in two parts—one part for your personal objectives, and one part for your professional objectives. Your three-year vision represents a stake in the ground for you. It is time-bound, and more specific than your longer-term vision. It represents progress toward your long-term vision, and it defines what greatness looks like for you three years from today. It may include elements of your long-term vision, and it may have elements that are not fleshed-out there.

EXERCISE #3A: THREE-YEAR PERSONAL VISION

Now that you have started thinking about the possibilities in your life, let's get specific. In the box below, first enter your age—three years from today. Time is passing!

Next, determine what you want your personal life to be like in three years. Consider the following areas, and any others that may come to mind:

Spouse ~ Family ~ Health ~ Spiritual ~ Social ~ Financial ~ Intellectual ~ Emotional ~ Life Style

Three-Year Personal Vision   Age: _55_

Financial - Have acquired a net income of £1m.
Home - Bought outright dream georgian house &
renovated it to a beautiful standard. + natural Pool
Health - Strong, healthy + competing in Ironman's. Bought girls childhood homes
Family - Successful, happy, healthy daughters.
Spiritual - meditating daily + developing deeper
insight into the nature of reality that sticks.
Intellectual - Co-written /authored 200 books.
and make time to continue to read + learn.
Emotional - Happy, grateful, content, peaceful
joyous + learnt to laugh a lot!
Lifestyle - Elegant, free, empowered, beautiful
furniture + paintings travel frequently - visit
kensington flat for events /galleries. + I love
travelling in my beautiful customised campervan.

EXERCISE #3B: THREE-YEAR BUSINESS VISION

Now that you have some clarity on what you want your personal life to look like in three years, let's take a look at your professional vision. Your career/business vision should align and enable your life vision. Your professional vision should financially fund your life vision, and it should provide the desired amount of free time. Further, your career should be enjoyable and rewarding in itself. The areas you focus on, and the work you choose to do, should be chosen to best support your life vision.

Consider the following questions:

What is your ideal profession? What areas do you excel in? What value do you create, and what difference do you make? Where will you feel most fulfilled? What will your income be? How much time off will you have? What position/role will you be playing? Will you lead others? What will your team look like?	If you are an entrepreneur: What space will you operate out of? Will you have multiple locations? What is your target market? What is your ideal client profile? What is your value offer? How many clients will you have in profile? What is your service model? How will you market? Will you be referral based?

Three-Year Business Vision

I have two businesses. Wellness + publishing. They often interrelate. My publishing business busines on fiction/non fiction/wellness + spirituality/ business children books. I take from what I know + what gives value + joy. I have a successful passive income + have co-author 200 books that brings in a monthly income approx £55,000 per month. I have brilliant feedback + the books are loved by many. I also teache spiritual business + run retreats where I share my wellness + confidence/empowering courses. I do a lot of book signings + visit schools.

For those of you in annualized organizations, or those with important annual personal objectives, an additional helpful step is to determine your 12-month vision. It often helps to view your annual objectives as your vision four 12 Week Years from today. Your 12-month vision should define the progress needed to be on-track with your three-year vision, and it should describe what greatness looks like for you 12 months from today.

EXERCISE #4: 12-MONTH VISION (OPTIONAL)

What will your personal and professional life look like at the end of the next 12 months? Identify where you need to be to stay on track with your three-year and long-term visions below:

12 Month Vision

It is June 20th 2023 and I have had an incredible year. I found the secret to unlocking my creative potential, believing in my power and seeing it reflect in my success. I have produced 100 books in the past year with 50% of them best sellers in their category. Squeelsy was finally introduced to the world. I have made an average monthly income of £300,000 but this is nearly £500,000 now. I have also found the magic ingredient to self-care + now exercise, yoga + weight train every day. I have completed my first half ironman. I continue to work hard to generate more books but I no longer contract. Arte has finished school and I now know I can support her + apple comfortably with their education. I have made £2.5 million this year and now have so many possibilities ahead. I have bought + created a beautiful customised Campervan + looking for a Georgian house that has its own water source. I feel deeply blessed + spend time each morning in spiritual practise.

COMMON VISION PITFALLS

Don't let these three common vision pitfalls derail your achievement:

Pitfall 1: Not Taking the Power of Vision Seriously

Some people, especially type A's, think that vision is fluff. Those who think about vision this way tend to leap past the question of purpose and dive into action. The problem is that when the going gets difficult, it is harder to stay committed to the work in the long run because there is no compelling reason—no persuasive "why." The behaviors associated with this pitfall are not keeping your vision in front of you, not aligning your plans with it, and not remembering what is in it.

Pitfall 2: Not Making Your Vision Meaningful to You

Sometimes we are superficial in crafting our vision. We capture what we think we want, or we capture what we think we are supposed to want, rather than capturing what is meaningful to us. Visioning takes time. Keep working on it until you have an emotional connection to it.

Pitfall 3: Making Your Vision Too Small

A small vision doesn't call on your best efforts. You don't have to reach, and you don't sacrifice your comfort. A small vision might be achievable, but you leave your best undelivered. To be most effective, your vision should make you feel uncomfortable— it should challenge you into doing things differently, and doing different things.

You've crafted your vision at this point and checked it to avoid making those common mistakes. Here are four important action steps to take to make your vision even more powerful:

Action 1: Share It with Others

By sharing your vision, you become committed to it. When you tell someone who is important to you what you want in life, you often feel more responsibility to act.

Action 2: Stay in Touch with Your Vision

Print it out, or make a copy, and keep it with you. Review it each morning. Update it every time that you discover ways to make it more vivid and meaningful to you. We suggest creating a 12WY Vision & Commitment Card. Go to 12weekyear.com/fieldguide.

Action 3: Connect Your Vision to Your Daily Actions

Each day is an opportunity to either make progress on your vision or to tread water. If you work from a plan that is aligned with your vision, you can be sure that you are acting on the most important things every day.

Action 4: Be Intentional

At the end of each day, take a few minutes to reflect on the progress that you made today. Did it move you forward, or was it filled with activity that wasn't related to your vision? Resolve to be intentional to make progress on your vision—what action will you take tomorrow?

Now armed with your vision for inspiration, it is time to begin the exciting process of creating your roadmap to the future of your dreams—your 12 Week Year Plan!

CHAPTER 2

Establishing Your Goals and Building Your Plan

In order to set up your 12 Week Year, you will need to establish specific 12 week goals and then build a 12 week tactical plan to achieve them.

Using your vision as your guide, set a specific and measurable goal (or goals), for the upcoming 12 Week Year. These goals should represent realistic progress toward your three-year personal and business visions, and your 12 month vision if you have one, and it should create a sense of excitement all on its own.

If you find that you need more than one goal, keep in mind that "less is more." It is important that you focus. With the 12 Week Year, our philosophy is this: *Let's be great at a few things, versus mediocre at many.* Too often people end up diffused, taking on more than they can effectively execute.

Once your 12 week goals are clear and focused, we move on to the second step, in which you will develop a tactical plan to achieve them. At this stage, keeping it simple is the best approach. For each goal, determine the "critical few" actions (tactics) that you will take to achieve your goal. Write these tactics in a way that clearly describes the actions you will need to take.

STARTING WITH THE END IN MIND

Figure 2.1 is a sample **12 Week Plan**. Refer to it as needed to help guide you as you write *your* 12 week plan. In this lesson, you will work to create a similar plan. There is no such thing as a perfect plan. Capture your best thinking—you can edit it later if needed as you execute your plan.

Get your free resources at www.12weekyear.com/fieldguide

12 WEEK GOALS

PERIOD GOALS
> Achieve Production Credit of $62,000
> Weigh 185 LBS by the end of the 12 Week Year

Your Plan is focused on a few goals – the critical areas where you would like to improve right away and to make progress towards your vision.

12 WEEK PLAN

GOAL #1: Achieve Production Credit of $62,000

Your Tactics describe the actions you will need to take to accomplish each goal.

KEY ACTIONS/TACTICS	WEEKS DUE
Enter all prospects into Contact Management System	1-12
Schedule 10 appointments per week	1-12
Conduct a minimum of 8 appointments per week	2-12
Schedule 4 two hour prospecting blocks each week	1-12
Identify 12 centers of influence (COI's)	1-2
Meet with 1 COI per week and ask for names	3-12

GOAL #2: Weigh 185 LBS by the end of the 12 Week Year

KEY ACTIONS/TACTICS	WEEKS DUE
Run 3 times/week for a min. of 3 miles/run weeks	2-12
Swim laps 2 times/week for a min. of 30 minutes/swim	3-12
Find an exercise buddy that lives nearby	1
Set exercise schedule with buddy that works for us both	1
Limit alcohol to Fri. night and Sat. – 2 drinks/night max	1-12

Figure 2.1 Sample 12 Week Plan

Well written 12 week plans have two levels of structure:

Level 1—The 12 Week Goal—this is *where* you want to be at the end of 12 weeks. It links to your vision, and represents the progress you intend to make toward it during this 12 week period. While you may have multiple goals, just remember, "less is more." The more focused your plan is, the more effective you will be.

Level 2—The Weekly Tactics—these are the *hows* (the actions you will take) to accomplish each goal. The tactics will guide you each week and help you to act. The way you write your tactics is important because if they are well written, they will greatly increase your chances of hitting your goals.

In general, it helps to think of your goals as outcomes (which you don't control) and your tactics as actions (which you *do* control).

The way that your plan is written has a huge impact on the effectiveness of your execution. Vague or poorly written goals and tactics will hinder you. Likewise, a well-constructed goal is clear and precise, thereby making implementation easier. Next are some tips for ensuring your goals are expressed for success.

WRITING EFFECTIVE GOALS

To be truly effective, there are five criteria to apply when constructing your goals:

Criteria 1: Make your goals specific and measurable.

For each goal, be sure to quantify and qualify what success looks like. Exactly how much money will you earn? How many pounds will you lose? The more specific you can be, the better!

Criteria 2: State each goal positively.

In general, it makes sense to focus on what you want to happen that is positive. For example: If your initial goal is "Achieve a 2% error rate," you really are not interested in *errors*, you are more interested in *accuracy*. Restate the goal as "Achieve a 98% accuracy rate."

Criteria 3: Ensure that each goal is a realistic stretch for you.

If you can accomplish the goal by doing very little differently, then you probably need to stretch more. If your goal is absolutely impossible, then back it off a little.

Criteria 4: Include accountability.

Take ownership of each of your goals. If you are not willing to sacrifice your comfort if necessary to reach your goal, then don't put it in your plan in the first place.

Criteria 5: Be time bound.

There is nothing like a deadline to get, and keep, things moving. Make sure to include a date by which your goal is to be reached.

Credit: David Carillet/Shutterstock.com.

We will say it again: how your plan is structured and written has a huge impact on your execution. Vague or poorly written goals will hinder effective execution. Likewise, a well-constructed goal is clear and precise, thereby making implementation easier.

Below, you will find some examples of well-written goals that apply these important criteria.

EXAMPLE 1

"Lose 10 lbs. and weigh 185."

This goal meets all the criteria: It is specific and measurable, stated positively, realistic stretch, time bound (by the end of the 12 Week Year), and accountability is implied—you are the one who must own it.

EXAMPLE 2

"Sell $50,000 in new business this 12 Week Year."

Again, this goal meets all the criteria.

A good goal supports good execution. It is easier to determine the tactics if the goal is well written. If the goal is vague, then identifying effective tactics becomes much more difficult (if not impossible.)

Okay, now it's *your* turn. On the following pages is a **12 Week Year Game Plan Worksheet**. Take sufficient time to develop your goals, and write them on the worksheet in the spaces provided. This is a process that likely will require you to do some editing, clarification, and refinement as you go. That's why we give you a chance to write your goals down before you restate them in your draft 12 Week Plan.

Be sure to not overload yourself and run the risk of diffusion. Remember—it is better to be great at a *few* things than mediocre at *many* things! Generally, we recommend having no more than one to three goals.

12 Week Year Game Plan Worksheet

For the 12 Week Year Ending 20 / 9 / 22, I will:

Goal 1: I will have published three books -
3 non-fiction. - with Passive income £6000

Goal 2: I will have completed my first
olympic triathlon

Goal 3: I will have created a panive
income stream of £6000 per month.
Completed KDI.

Barriers and Challenges

As you consider these goals, take a few minutes to capture the top two to three things that might keep you from hitting your goals within 12 weeks. Consider both internal and external factors. Internal factors might be things like easily distracted, fears, or lack of knowledge. Examples of external factors might be competing priorities at work, vacation time scheduled, or being short staffed. My challenges for this 12 week period are:

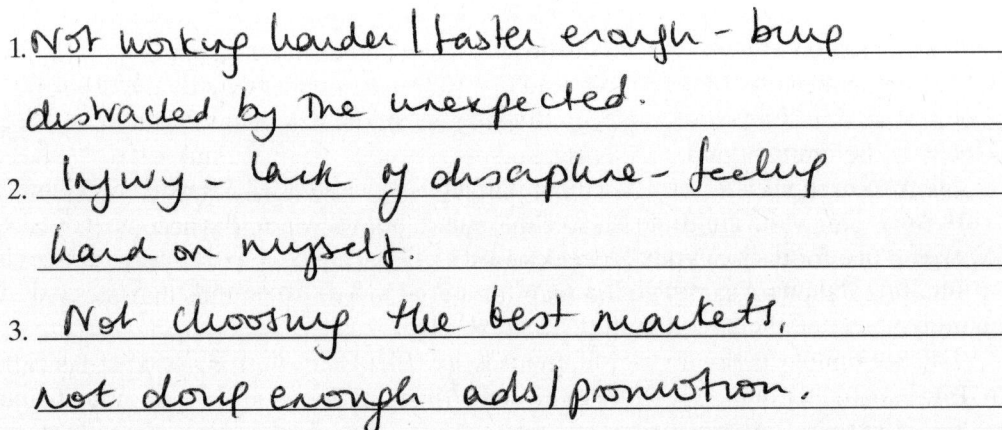

1. Not working harder/faster enough - being distracted by the unexpected.

2. Injury - lack of discipline - feeling hard on myself.

3. Not choosing the best markets, not doing enough ads/promotion.

Given the things that might get in the way for you during these 12 weeks, identify some ways that you might increase your odds by addressing these factors in your plan. For example, if you are taking a two-week vacation, you might want to schedule your tactics not to come due at that time, or if you are easily distracted you might consider ways to isolate yourself from interruptions:

Ways to Overcome the Challenges as You Plan

Put 2 hrs aside each day for focused work.
Don't have phone on.
- Injury - Slow + consistent discipline -
build slowly - don't be impatient
anti inflammatory diet
- focus on markets - be head rather
than heart to begin with

12 WEEK PLAN TACTICS

First decide which of the possible 12 week goals that you just outlined above will be included in your 12 Week Plan—remember, less is more.

For each 12 week goal that you decide to pursue, refine the goal to meet the criteria outlined earlier, and then restate the goal in the blank planning forms starting on page 19.

For each goal, the next step is to determine the minimum number of tactics needed to reach it, and no more. We recommend that you mind-map each goal to help you identify potential tactics to reach the goal.

If you are familiar with the brainstorming technique of mind-mapping, you know of its power to generate ideas. Many people tend to solve problems linearly: step a, step b, step c, and so on. Such a linear approach can limit the number of ideas generated. With mind mapping, you avoid the limits of linear thinking, and access more creative thinking, which is where breakthroughs come from. If you are not familiar with mind mapping, you might download a mind-mapping software program to experiment, but all you really need is a blank sheet of paper—one for each of your 12 week goals.

Figure 2.2 shows a sample mind map for a goal to lose 10 pounds that you can use as a guide.

In this example, there are four main ideas: exercise, diet, coaching, and medical advice. Each main idea is then built out with some related ideas.

Keep in mind that every mind map is different—they reflect the way that you brainstorm. Don't worry if your maps are not as structured as the example—in fact, they may not have any discernible structure at all—the important thing is to capture your ideas.

First, write your goal in the middle of a blank sheet of paper. In the following example, that goal is stated as "Lose 10 lbs." Next, brainstorm all of the things that you could do to achieve that goal and write them down around the center goal and circle them as unique ideas. For those ideas that are related, connect them with lines (see the example). Write all of your ideas down—you will narrow them down later. Also, don't worry about writing them out as actions—just capture the ideas.

As you build out your mind map, you can expect to get stuck a couple of times. Often your most creative and powerful ideas come after getting stuck once or twice. Be patient and you will likely identify the tactics needed to hit your goals.

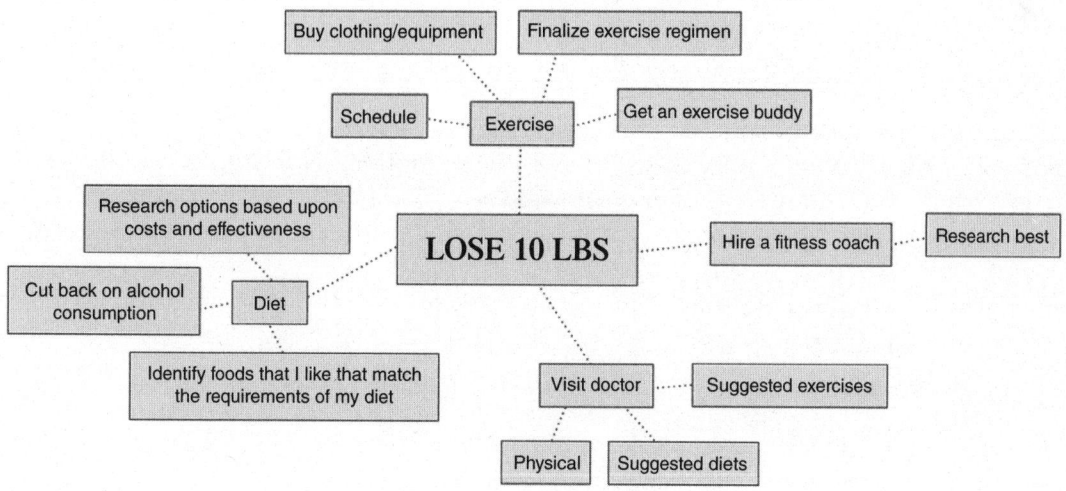

Figure 2.2 A mind map to lose 10 pounds.

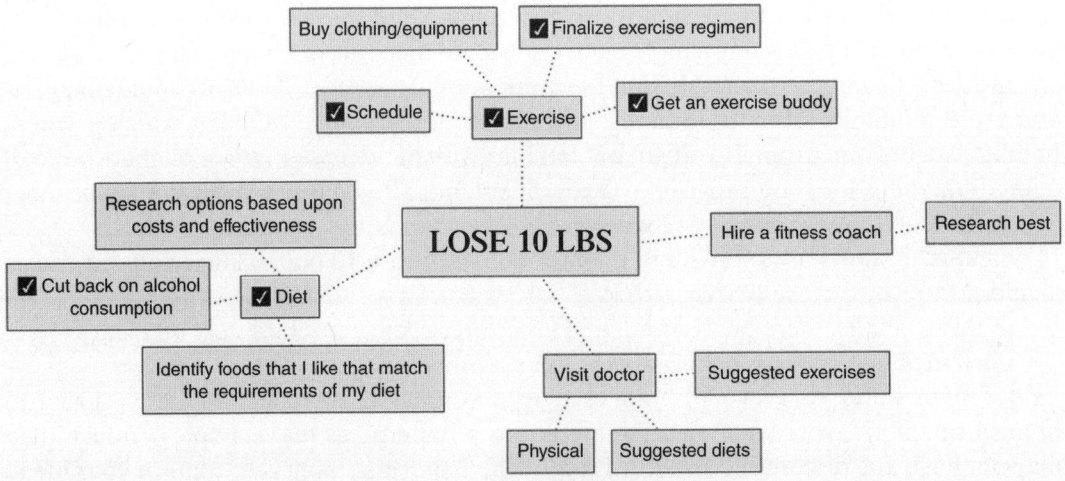

Figure 2.3 The revised mind map to lose 10 pounds.

Once you have brainstormed your action ideas for each of your goals, it's time to pick the most impactful ones and then rewrite them to conform to the criteria for well-written tactics (see further on).

First, select the best ideas (the ones that will have the biggest impact on hitting your goal) from your mind map. You likely won't need them all. In fact, less is more (sound familiar?). If you can hit your goal by executing just the most powerful one of your mind-mapped ideas, then stop there. If not, add the second most impactful, and if those two are all you need, then stop there. If not, keep going until you have just enough of the right tactics to hit your goal, and then stop.

Using the earlier example for losing 10 pounds, the following tactics (see Figure 2.3) were selected:

The selected ideas, "exercise," "schedule," "get an exercise buddy," "finalize exercise regimen," "diet," and "cut back on alcohol consumption," are still not well-written tactics—they will require some additional work.

Now it's time to rewrite these ideas to conform to the criteria for well-written tactics:

Tactic Criterion 1: Conform to the criteria for well-written 12 week goals

Tactic Criterion 2: Start with an action verb and written as a complete sentence

Tactic Criterion 3: Can be executed as written, in the week that they are due, without significant prework.

Tactic Criterion 4: Specify frequency and due dates

Below are the goal and ideas selected in figure 2.3 re-written to conform to the criteria for well written goals and tactics.

12 Week Goal: "Weigh 185 lbs. by the end of the 12 Week Year"

Tactic 1: Run three times/week for a minimum of three miles/run, weeks 2–12

Tactic 2: Swim laps two times/week for a minimum of 30 minutes/swim, weeks 3–12

Tactic 3: Find an exercise buddy that lives nearby, week 1

Tactic 4: Set exercise schedule with buddy that works for us both, week 1

Tactic 5: Limit alcohol to Friday and Saturday nights – two drinks/night max, wks 1–12

There are other ways that these tactics could have been written. In some cases, mind-mapped ideas can be broken into two or more tactics ("finalize exercise routine" became "swim laps" and "run"). In some cases, ideas can collapse into fewer tactics. The important thing is to write the tactics to conform to the criteria above.

Even with your best thinking, your tactics may or may not work as you intend. The best way to improve them is to execute the plan, see what happens, and adjust the 12 week plan as needed.

Goal 1: Publish 3 books with a passive income of £6000+

Tactics | | **Week Due**
A: Generate book ideas by Week 1 | 1 20/6
B: Market research × 3. | 1
C: Hire writer + designer × 3. | 2 27/6
D: Create 3× brief | 2
E: Proof Read. × 3 | 6–7 1st Aug
F: Publish books. × 3. | 8 – 15/Aug
G: Advertise | 8–12

For Goal 1, what support or assistance might you need from others to increase your odds of success?

Keep checking KDI facebook page. Attend Q+A - Tues/wed.
Mgkt need to invest in KX10.

Goal 2: _Complete KDI course._

Tactics		**Week Due**
A:	Commit to 2 hours per day	1 - 14
B:	Do all the assignments	
C:	Attend all Q & A's.	1 - 12
D:	Look for a buddy on facebook	2
E:	Create plan./timetable.	1.
F:		
G:		

For Goal 2, what support or assistance might you need from others to increase your odds of success?

Make sure I do these when not interrupted. Need to rise early to put in - create timetable.

Goal 3: _Completed olympic triathlon._

Tactics		**Week Due**
A:	Create exercise timetable	1
B:	Create food plan.	1

C: ~~Foto~~ Set up dining room　　　　　　　　　1
D: ~~Follow~~ metabolic exercises　　　　　　　1-12
E: ~~Follow~~ Yoga on Vaha　　　　　　　　　1-12
F: 3 × swims 1500 m per week　　　　　　　1-12
G: 2 × bike　2 × run.　　　　　　　　　　1-6.
　　2 × bike　3 × run　　　　　　　　　　　@ 7-12

For Goal 3, what support or assistance might you need from others to increase your odds of success?

Injury - Plan - slow + steady.
Lose weight
Be organised - Plans essential
Print out plans
Re do vision board.

To be sure that you leverage your vision as you execute your plan, take a few minutes to capture how your current 12 week goals represent progress toward your vision (you likely won't make progress on everything in your vision in 12 weeks, but by thinking through how your 12 week goal moves you toward your long-term aspirations, it will help you to take action even in the times you might not *feel* like it):

Edit vision board.

COMMON PITFALLS AND SUCCESS TIPS

Don't let these five common pitfalls derail your achievement:

Pitfall 1: Not Aligning with a Longer-Term Vision

It is important that your 12 week goals and your plan are aligned with, and an extension of, your longer-term vision. When you set your goals, be certain that they are connected to your vision. Determine where you need to be at the end of 12 weeks to be on pace with your vision.

Pitfall 2: Not Staying Focused

Focus is critical. If you establish too many goals, you end up with too many priorities and too many tactics to effectively execute. Everything cannot be a priority. You will need to say "no" to some things in order to be great at the things that matter most. It takes courage to limit your focus to a few key areas. Remember, each 12 weeks is a new year. Imagine if every 12 weeks you identified one or two key areas and went after those with passion and focus. Then, at the end of that 12 week period, you identified one or two new areas to focus on. The 12 Week Year is designed to help you focus on a few key areas and make significant progress in a short period of time.

Pitfall 3: Not Making the Tough Choices

For each goal, it's not uncommon to identify 8, 10, or more tactics (actions) you could take to "move the ball down the field." In most cases, implementing every tactic you can think of is not necessary and, in fact, can be a hindrance. Although it's helpful to brainstorm all the tactics you can think of, that doesn't mean you have to implement all of them. Too many tactics can spread you too thin and leave you feeling overwhelmed. On the flip side though, there is no "right" number of tactics. As with your goals, less is more. If you can accomplish the goal with four tactics, then you don't need five. Brainstorm all the tactics you can, and then select the critical few.

Tip 1: Keep It Simple

The task of planning can become very complex. In some companies, entire departments exist for the sole

Credit: Mikadun/Shutterstock.com.

purpose of drafting strategic plans. For the purposes of the 12 Week Year, keep it simple. If you feel like it's getting too complicated, it probably is. Focus on a few key areas and the actions you can take to hit your goals.

Tip 2: Make It Meaningful

What you build your plan around must be the most important items or the plan will have little traction for you in the implementation phase. Too often people build their plan around the goals that someone else thinks are important. Although executing your plan is not complex, it is not necessarily easy either. If your plan is not meaningful to you, then you will struggle to execute it. Be certain that you focus on the areas that matter most.

CHAPTER 3

Making and Keeping 12 Week Commitments

---

*C*ommitment, the second of the three principles of the 12 Week Year, is defined as "the state of being bound emotionally or intellectually to some course of action." A commitment is a conscious decision to take specific action to create a desired result.

Commitments are powerful. In a way, commitment is your accountability projected into the future. You decide beforehand that you will do whatever it takes to reach your goal. The more accountable you are, the more likely you will be to meet your commitments.

Commitment: (n) 1: "The state of being bound emotionally or intellectually to some course of action."

We all have examples in our lives of the power of commitment—a time when we locked on to a goal or objective and were willing to do whatever it took to reach it. Think back on a time like that for you. What were you feeling? How did it feel to reach your goal? How did it make you feel about your ability to reach other goals?

How did your commitment affect your daily decisions and actions—especially when you were tempted to give up?

Credit: Bojanovic/Shutterstock.com.

Get your free resources at www.12weekyear.com/fieldguide

Commitments are a powerful tool. Keeping commitments with *others* builds relationships. Keeping commitments with *yourself* builds integrity and self-respect. In this field guide, we will focus on keeping commitments with yourself.

———

BENEFITS OF KEEPING COMMITMENTS

Take a few minutes right now to think about two personal commitments that you have made and kept with yourself. Record the commitments below.

Commitment #1: _Raising my children to the best of my ability_

Commitment #2: _keeping a peaceful home_

Now, think about what the results were for you when you kept these commitments. How did you feel about yourself? Was it easier to make and keep other self-promises as a result of keeping these? How did you feel about your ability to do what it takes to get the result—no matter what?

Capture your thoughts below:

I am proud of how I have raised the girls. Not easier to keep others. Its hardwork but because it aligns with my deepest values, it is who I am.

Many times, commitments are made more arduous by the time frame in which the commitment is undertaken. It is difficult to commit to anything for a lifetime. Even keeping a promise for an entire year can be challenging. With the 12 Week Year, you are not asked to make a lifetime or annual commitment, but rather 12 week commitments. It is much more feasible to establish and keep a 12 week commitment than an annual promise. At the end of the 12 weeks, you will reassess your commitments and begin again.

By making and keeping 12 week commitments, you will strengthen your ability to follow through with your self-promises, which can create a true breakthrough in your life.

Below is a **Commitment Worksheet**. For most people, their 12 week plan focuses primarily on their business or career. The commitment section is a place where you can address some of the other personal areas where you desire to make progress.

To complete the worksheet below, follow these four simple instructions:

Commitment

1. Determine a few personal **goals** that would represent real breakthroughs for you that fall into one of the categories in the commitment wheel (spiritual, spouse/relationship, physical, personal, business, or family). Write these goals in the column labeled "Goal Statements." Remember to state these goals positively! For example, say "I want to weigh X pounds" rather than "I want to lose X pounds."

2. Identify the **key action(s)** that will get you there. In the example above, "I want to weigh X pounds," you might choose to limit calories or workout each day. Pick one of the actions—the action you believe will have the greatest impact on you achieving the goal. It's important to note that we are not saying that this is necessarily the *only* action that you will need to take, merely the one with the greatest impact. Ideally, this action is something that you can engage in daily or weekly. Write one action for each goal in the column labeled "Commitment Action."

3. Consider what **costs** you will have to pay to take that action every week and write them in the "Costs" area. For example, costs of working out every day might include: giving up TV or golf, less time with your family, or getting up earlier. Costs of dieting might include: giving up some favorite foods, reducing the number of times you eat out, or eating smaller portions.

4. Circle those Commitment Actions for which you are willing to pay the price. They will become your commitments for the next 12 weeks.

The 12 Week Year is a system that you can use to accomplish goals in any area of your life. As you consider what you want to include as commitments, look at the categories on the right. Any area in our lives can be a source of energy if they are going well, or a drain on our energy if they are not where we want them to be. Take a few minutes to identify a few areas that you are interested in getting better and use those areas to complete the following table.

Commitment Wheel

Commitment Worksheet

Goal Statement	Commitment Action	Costs
Example: I want to weigh 170 pounds.	Work out daily.	Get less sleep. Do it when I'm tired.
I want to weigh 147 lbs.	Work out daily. Follow Plan.	Up early. No excuses. Sacrifice social outings for early morning.
I want to read my book club books.	20 minutes audible.	No excuse on train journey.
Meditate + complete mantra.	2 x daily	Early rising Leave an hour before sleep.
Update website with videos.	Call Clive + sort.	~~New~~ Find 2 hrs in a week

"The quality of a person's life is in direct proportion to their commitment to excellence, regardless of their chosen field of endeavor."

– Vince Lombardi

PITFALLS TO AVOID

Don't let these three common pitfalls trip you up:

Pitfall 1: Missing a Commitment Once and Giving Up

Sometimes life gets in the way and you are not able to meet your commitments and you disappoint yourself and others. When this happens, it is important to get right back on the horse that threw you. Don't give up!

Pitfall 2: Failing to Confront Missed Commitments

A commitment isn't an interest that is abandoned when it gets difficult. When things get in the way of meeting a commitment, it is important to dig into *why*. Confront the breakdown right away and recommit to paying the price. In that way, you grow your ability to make and meet commitments in the future.

Pitfall 3: Not Valuing Keeping Your Word

Sometimes you make promises that you cannot keep. Many times, we know this before we make the promise. We avoid short-term relationship pain by saying "yes" when we should say "no." The problem is that when you break your word, that's when you damage relationships. People begin to feel that they cannot trust you. When you value keeping your word, you avoid making promises that you know you cannot or will not keep.

Credit: sportpoint/Shutterstock.com.

Get your free resources at www.12weekyear.com/fieldguide

CHAPTER 4

Installing Process Control

Process Control leverages a set of tools and events that will help you work your plan and stay with it for the duration of your 12 Week Year. These include a Weekly Plan, Weekly Accountability Meetings, Daily Huddles, 12 Week Themes, and Celebrations. Each of these elements of Process Control are based on research on change, and will help you to execute at your best and to overcome the obstacles you will encounter on the way.

WEEKLY PLAN

At the beginning of each week, you will create a weekly plan that contains the actions (tactics) and commitments that are due this week from your 12 Week Plan.

The Weekly Plan is such a powerful tool because it simply and effectively translates the entire 12 Week Plan into more manageable and focused daily and weekly actions. It is the instrument that organizes and drives your week, becoming, in effect, your "game plan" for those seven days.

Your weekly plan is not a "to-do" list; rather, it reflects the critical strategic activity that needs to take place this week to achieve your 12 week goals. The sections of the weekly plan address the core elements that drive performance and life balance.

Each week, you will create a weekly plan derived from your 12 Week Plan (see Figure 4.1). At the end of this field guide we have included a copy of our paper-based system for you to use. The paper system contains a 12 Week Year Game Plan (your 12 week plan), and 13 individual weekly plans.

Get your free resources at www.12weekyear.com/fieldguide

WEEKLY PLAN & SCORECARD - WEEK 1

12 WEEK GOAL: Achieve Production Credit of $62,000 and Weigh 185 LBS by the end of the 12WY

KEY ACTIONS/TACTICS List of your key actions and the day you wish to complete them	WHO	DAY
Enter all prospects into Contact Management System	BM	Mon
Schedule 10 appointments per week	BM	Tues
Schedule 4 two hour prospecting blocks each week	BM	Wed
Identify 12 centers of influence (COI's)	BM	Thu
Find an exercise buddy that lives nearby	BM	Tue
Set exercise schedule with buddy that works for us both	BM	Mon
Limit alcohol to Fri. night and Sat. – 2 drinks/night max	BM	Mon-Sun

TIME BLOCK Set up your time blocks for the week	DAY/TIME
Strategic Block	Tues 8-11am
Buffer Blocks	Mon 7:30 - 8am Fri 4:30 - 5pm

"An aspiration or desire means little without a plan to get there"

WEEKLY SCORECARD
Tactics completed / Total Tactics × 100 = your percentage

$$7 \div 9 \times 100 = 78\%$$

12 WEEK GOALS

PERIOD GOALS
> Achieve Production Credit of $62,000
> Weigh 185 LBS by the end of the 12 Week Year

12 WEEK PLAN

GOAL #1: Achieve Production Credit of $62,000

KEY ACTIONS/TACTICS	WEEKS DUE
Enter all prospects into Contact Management System	1-12
Schedule 10 appointments per week	1-12
Conduct a minimum of 8 appointments per week	2-12
Schedule 4 two hour prospecting blocks each week	1-12
Identify 12 centers of influence (COI's)	1-2
Meet with 1 COI per week and ask for names	3-12

GOAL #2: Weigh 185 LBS by the end of the 12 Week Year

KEY ACTIONS/TACTICS	WEEKS DUE
Run 3 times/week for a min. of 3 miles/run weeks	2-12
Swim laps 2 times/week for a min. of 30 minutes/swim	3-12
Find an exercise buddy that lives nearby	1
Set exercise schedule with buddy that works for us both	1
Limit alcohol to Fri. night and Sat. – 2 drinks/night max	1-12

Figure 4.1 Your weekly plan (right) is derived from your 12 Week Plan (left).

Each week, take a few minutes to plan your week using the tools provided.

WEEKLY PLAN & SCORECARD - WEEK 1

12 Week Goal

In this section of the Weekly Plan and Scorecard, you will see your 12 Week Goal. In our example, Susan's goal is $62,000.

12 WEEK GOAL: Achieve Production Credit of $62,000 and Weigh 185 LBS by the end of the 12WY

KEY ACTIONS/TACTICS List of your key actions and the day you wish to complete them	WHO	DAY
Enter all prospects into Contact Management System	BM	Mon
Schedule 10 appointments per week	BM	Tues
Schedule 4 two hour prospecting blocks each week	BM	Wed
Identify 12 centers of influence (COI's)	BM	Thu
Find an exercise buddy that lives nearby	BM	Tue
Set exercise schedule with buddy that works for us both	BM	Mon
Limit alcohol to Fri. night and Sat. – 2 drinks/night max	BM	Mon-Sun

Key Actions/Tactics

This section contains the tactics from your 12 Week Plan that are due this week, as well as your personal commitments.

Time Block

This section is where you will note your strategic blocks and buffer blocks for the week. Read on for a detailed discussion of time blocking, which can be found in Chapter 6.

TIME BLOCK Set up your time blocks for the week	DAY/TIME
Strategic Block	Tues 8-11am
Buffer Blocks	Mon 7:30 - 8am Fri 4:30 - 5pm

"An aspiration or desire means little without a plan to get there"

~ Unknown

WEEKLY SCORECARD Tactics completed / Total Tactics × 100 = your percentage			
	7 ÷ 9	× 100 =	78%

Taken together, these sections constitute your weekly plan. Each week you will create a written weekly plan that arises from your 12 Week Plan. Your weekly plan becomes your simple-to-follow road map to success, ensuring that you complete, in a timely manner, the critical near-term activities necessary to ultimately achieve your long-term goals.

The weekly plan prompts you to take action on your most important tasks every day of the week, in spite of all the distractions and interruptions that you encounter. It is a critical part of your weekly execution discipline.

WEEKLY ACCOUNTABILITY MEETING (WAM)

If you search for "peer support" on Google, you will get page after page after page of websites that offer help in difficult times. Peer support is a proven and powerful way to increase your odds of success—not only in times of difficulty, but in times of opportunity as well.

Peers can have an enormous impact on your thinking, your actions, and your results. A peer is someone whom *you* see as equal or similar to you in important ways such as common profession, performance levels, perspectives, and values. A peer can offer you valuable insights and increase your motivation to act on those insights.

The Weekly Accountability Meeting (WAM) is a powerful way to apply the concept of peer support and is a critical element of Process Control. A WAM is a short meeting, typically held on Monday morning, after everyone has had a chance to plan their week. This meeting lasts approximately 15–30 minutes and is a forum designed to foster personal accountability. This is not a punitive session where we try to "hold people accountable" and dole out negative consequences for those who are faltering. On the contrary, the WAM is a session where each individual holds themselves accountable.

You will want to select two or three other people with whom you can hold a WAM. When selecting a WAM buddy, pick individuals who are goal driven and will be supportive. A WAM can be conducted in person or over the phone. Here is a simple example of a WAM agenda:

WAM AGENDA

Individual Report Out

- Results: Actual to Goal
- Weekly Execution Score
- What's working, where I'm struggling, action commitment this week
- Group challenges, feedback, encouragement

Close and Identify Follow-Ups

Each WAM member comes prepared to report out to the group on how they scored by goal, what their average weekly score is by goal, what their progress is in terms of their lead and lag metrics, and what they will do this week given what happened last week.

To be most effective, the WAMs should have operating rules that everyone buys into. We recommend that you share your 12 Week Goals and Plans with the other members of your WAM and identify areas where you would like their focus each week.

One of our clients has a WAM charter that, among other things, allows only one missed meeting without a valid reason. Every member of the WAM has to sign the charter to be a member. That WAM takes the process seriously and they get serious results—they are the top performers in their firm.

Take a few minutes and capture the rules that you would like your WAM to adhere to so as to ensure that it creates value for the participants:

- _____

- _____

- _____
- _____
- _____
- _____

Research on change shows that you are about seven times more likely to stick with the execution of your plan over the long haul if you attend a weekly meeting with your peers to review your progress and your execution.

The reason for this incredible bump in "stick-to-it-ness" when people are in peer to peer groups is that individuals tend to give themselves *huge passes* if they fall short on their execution because they tend to judge themselves on their intentions. Peers, however, cannot see your intentions. Since they don't know your intentions, all they can evaluate are your results. And if you haven't executed well, that is how they will confront you—on the gap between what you said you were going to do and what you actually did. That is uncomfortable, and discomfort can motivate you to take action.

The WAM focus on your actions and your results is what keeps you honest with yourself. Knowing that you will be meeting with your peers next week to review what you did this week has a positive effect on your actions. You are much more likely to take the extra effort to get things done this week if you have a WAM next week.

As a member of a WAM, it is your duty to press in and support the other members. If someone is not prepared, have the courage to ask them to step out, get their numbers, and then come back. If someone in your WAM is scoring poorly, ask them what is keeping them from executing and what they plan to do differently this week to get back on track.

You have to continually fight the desire to be nice and to not make anyone else in your WAM uncomfortable. Remember why you are in the WAM in the first place—to help each other hit your 12 week goals—not to be someone's friend.

If others are not being totally honest, or are not taking ownership, think about what you *can* do rather than complain about what they are *not* doing. Ask for their feedback and ideas. Admit your performance breakdowns and genuinely seek input in the WAM.

—

DAILY HUDDLES

The Daily Huddle is a five-minute, stand-up meeting that occurs first thing every morning, preferably at the same time. Typically, daily huddles are met with push back. "We're too busy!" "That's crazy—we already have too many unproductive meetings!" Don't be deterred. We're talking about a meeting that lasts the equivalent of a bathroom break.

Daily Huddles work best with no more than three participants. The Daily Huddle agenda is brief: Yesterday's accomplishments and today's intentions.

---

12 WEEK THEME

A 12 Week Theme is an organizing theme that aligns with, and reinforces, your priorities and goals. A theme helps generate interest, maintain focus, and encourage action. The most effective themes are derived from your 12 Week Plan. Example themes include: "Own It," "Face Your Fears," "Personal Best," "Gratitude," and "Service Excellence." Ideally, the theme creates some emotional excitement and connection. The key to a good theme is that it is motivating.

Let's brainstorm some 12 Week Themes! Have fun with it! What can you come up with? List a few possibilities below:

Overcoming fear.

Stepping into my power!

Great! Now, it's time to actually *select* your first 12 Week Year Theme. What will it be?

My 12-Week Theme will be:

Stepping into my power!

_____

_____

_____

12 WEEK YEAR CELEBRATIONS

With the 12 Week Year we treat every 12 weeks as a year. Just like you used to do at the end of a calendar year, you take a holiday and celebrate after each 12 Week Year. In the book *The 12 Week Year,* there is a chapter dedicated to the thirteenth week. The thirteenth week is a flex week that is used to plan the next 12 Week Year and celebrate the progress and success of the current 12 weeks. If you've struggled, you might not have a big celebration. Conversely, if you had a breakthrough year, then you might take the entire week off.

The end of each 12 weeks is a time to reward yourself for the work you've done (Figure 4.2). Take a few minutes and determine how you would like to celebrate at the end of this 12 Week Year. Identify something that you find motivating and inspiring—a true reward.

Figure 4.2 Time to celebrate!

Credit: wavebreakmedia/Shutterstock.com.

IN RECOGNITION OF MY HARD WORK AND SUCCESSES THIS 12 WEEK YEAR, I WILL REWARD MYSELF BY DOING THE FOLLOWING:

Enjoy a spa day

_____

_____

_____

_____

_____

What we celebrate, and what we recognize, reinforces to ourselves and to others what we value. It may not be obvious, but celebration is a vital part of a good execution system.

Many of our clients are intentional about leveraging the power of celebration. One client of ours takes off the time after a successful 12 Week Year to go skiing for a week in Colorado, or to just get away, if it's not ski season.

Other celebrations are low-key, such as a long weekend away with the family, or a "staycation" to relax and recharge. Sometimes our clients will reward themselves with a "gift" that is meaningful to them—but only if they hit their 12 week goals. Think about something that you have always wanted (maybe something that you listed on your Have—Do—Be chart) and plan to reward yourself!

For a team, the key is to find a celebration that your team appreciates. One client of ours has an awards banquet that recognizes top performers for the 12 weeks.

STAY FOCUSED

Don't get overwhelmed with the five tools of Process Control! *It is not necessary for you to implement all of these tools and events in your first week of the 12 Week Year.* A more manageable approach might be to layer in one event each week or each month until you are fully utilizing the system.

However, there are two elements of Process Control that are part of your Weekly Execution Routine—and that routine is essential for each day of your 12 Week Year. Those tools are your weekly plan and the Weekly Accountability Meeting.

Once we introduce Scorekeeping in the next chapter, we will come back to these two tools and tie everything together.

COMMON PITFALLS AND SUCCESS TIPS

Don't let these common process control pitfalls rob you of success:

Pitfall 1: Not Planning Each Week

We all want to get off to a fast start each week. For many, Monday is a stress-filled day where they feel behind from the moment the day begins. It's natural to want to get the day started. Often, we just jump right in with email, voicemail, and whatever else may be awaiting us.

In addition to just diving into our week, lots of "things" can get in the way of us taking time to plan the week. Maybe "it" has even happened to you!

No time for it—we think that we're just too busy and that we'll get to it later, but later never comes.

Don't need it—the misguided thinking that somehow, you're the exception and don't need a game plan for the week. Watch how quickly the time slips away!

I'm above it—thinking that a Weekly Plan is for beginners, that someone in your position doesn't need it.

Already know it—the thinking that you already know what you need to do, so there's no benefit to writing it down or planning things out.

Don't want to be accountable for it—for some, working from a written weekly plan creates a level of discomfort because it continually reminds them when they are not doing what they know they should be doing.

Pitfall 2: Including All Your Tasks

The Weekly Plan does not contain everything you do in your job, just the strategic items from your 12 Week Plan. You should have a separate sheet with "to do" items and callbacks. Do not dilute your plan by adding all the lower-level activities that you do in the course of your day. Keep the Weekly Plan for just strategic items and commitments.

Pitfall 3: Assuming That Each Week Is the Same

Another mistake that many make is assuming that each week has the same activity so they create one Weekly Plan and then copy it each week. It's highly possibly that many of your weeks look similar. It's unlikely that all 12 weeks have the exact same activities due. Even if you are the statistical exception, the benefit of spending five to 10 minutes each week to set up your week pays big dividends.

Pitfall 4: Adding Tactics Weekly

Keep in mind that Weekly Plan is essentially a 1/12th slice of your 12 Week Plan. Occasionally, you may add a tactic to your Weekly Plan. However, this should be the exception. Most new tactics should be added to the 12 Week Plan first, and then flow through to the Weekly Plan. This prevents you from getting drawn into urgent activities that are not necessarily strategic.

Here are two tips to help you succeed.

Tip 1: Use the Weekly Plan to Guide Your Day

Once you've created your Weekly Plan, you will want to use it daily to keep you on track with the activities that are most important to achieving your goals. Check in with your Weekly Plan first thing each morning, once or twice throughout the day, and before you go home. When you learn to guide your daily activity based on your Weekly Plan is the moment when you will begin to experience true breakthrough performance.

Tip 2: Making It Part of Your Routine

Each of us has a routine. Routines are an important part of consistent success. Make the decision right now to incorporate the Weekly Plan into your daily and weekly routine.

CHAPTER 5

Scorekeeping

Measurement drives execution. It is the anchor of reality. To create your best results, you will need to track your 12 Week Year results daily, weekly, and monthly! Without measurement, there is no way to react quickly enough when things are not working to ensure that you hit your 12 week goals.

Measurement tells you how you are doing—how your actions are impacting the world. Without effective metrics, you lack the important information you need to make intelligent business decisions. To make the 12 Week Year work for you, you will need to measure both *lead* and *lag indicators*. Lead indicators are measures that show early progress toward the end result, while lag indicators often *are* the end results.

When you realize that a single week is the equivalent of a month in a 12 Week Year, the need to track lead and lag measures is apparent—a week lost is a month lost—track your numbers!

Step One is to develop a set of *key measures* that are a mix of lead and lag indicators. An example of a good mix of lead and lag measures for a sales goal might be referrals (lead), inquiries (lead), sales in dollars (lag), units sold (lag), and units ordered (lag). Lead and lag measures are important, but don't get carried away with too many metrics. Pick just the top one or two of each for you to track.

If you want to lose weight, a great lead indicator might be the number of hours that you exercise each week. A great lag indicator might be waist size or pounds lost. By tracking these indicators, you can determine each week if you are on track to hit, or miss, your goals.

Get your free resources at www.12weekyear.com/fieldguide

Capture the Lead and Lag measures for each of your goals below:

Goal One: Publish Three books.

Lead measures (early measures of progress):

1. 3x outlines Complete
2. Designers + writers ~~too~~ hired
3. Drafts returned for proof reading

Lag measures (late measures of progress):

1. 3 books Published
2. Positive Reviews
3. Ads in place.

Goal Two: Complete Course. KD1

Lead measures (early measures of progress):

1. 14 hours Committed to course per week
2. Attend all live sessions
3. Find a buddy

Lag measures (late measures of progress):

1. All modules complete
2. Assignment complete
3. Bonus material actioned.

Goal Three: _Complete stadard triathlon_

Lead measures (early measures of progress):

1. _7x daily training sessions   x7._
2. _Food Plan daul   1 Juice Per day   x7._
3. _2x healthy meals per day_

Lag measures (late measures of progress):

1. _- Lost 28 Pounds_
2. _- Successful finish with no cyfing_
3. _— High energy / feeling sharp_

We recommend that you track lead and lag numbers weekly and make them visible in a place that you (and your team, if you have one) see them often. Many of our clients use white boards to do this. Figure 5.1 shows a sample white board.

WEEKLY EXECUTION SCORES AND LEAD MEASURES												
WEEK	**1**	**2**	**3**	**4**	**5**	**6**	**7**	**8**	**9**	**10**	**11**	**12**
WEEKLY SCORE	80	70	65	75	85	90	85	87	82	80	75	84
AVERAGE SCORE	80	75	72	73	75	78	79	80	80	80	80	80
WEEKLY OPENERS	4	6	3	0	6	4	2	7	3	12	0	1
OPENERS TO DATE	4	10	13	13	19	23	25	32	35	47	47	48

LAG MEASURES												
GOAL 1 $	500	380	765	1670	100	564	0	823	1100	453	200	763
PTD $	500	880	1645	3315	3415	3979	3979	4802	5902	6355	6555	7118

Figure 5.1 An example of recording lead and lag numbers.

At the top of the example, the weekly execution score and a lead indicator (opening meetings with prospects) are tracked. At the bottom of the board a lag measure (closed sales measured in dollars) are tracked. By tracking these numbers, you know where you are every week.

Step Two is to track how well you execute your tactics each week. In addition to your other key measures, it's critical that you also measure your **execution effectiveness**. Establishing a metric that allows you to know each week how well you executed your tactics is essential. This is because you have more control over your actions than you do your outcomes. Your 12 week outcomes are created by your daily and weekly actions. To determine your weekly execution score, calculate the percentage of tactics that were due in a given week that were completed. If you have 10 tactics due, and you executed 8 of them, your score is 80% that week.

SUCCESS TIP

We have found that if you accomplish an average of 80% or more of your weekly tactics over the 12 Week Year, then, in most cases, you will reach your goal.

Step Three is to **pay attention**. Each week, take some time to review your metrics. Are there any performance breakdowns? Are you making good progress on your lead indicators? Are your lag indicators on pace to hit your 12 week goals? What do you need to do to keep up the momentum or to get back on track?

SUCCESS TIP

Keep track of your average weekly score and update it weekly. If you are scoring well—80% or higher on average—and your lead and lag metrics are not where they should be—change your plan. If you are not scoring well, don't change your plan. Instead, determine what's keeping you from working your plan and completing your tactics.

Once you have determined your metrics and are tracking them weekly, here are some tips to make your metrics work for you:

1. Review your weekly score and your results (lead and lag indicators) in your Weekly Accountability Meeting (WAM).

2. Commit to make progress each week. Maybe you can't get from 45% to 80% in one week, but you can move from 45% to 55%.

3. Remember that a score of less than 80% isn't necessarily bad. A score of 65% might be an improvement in activity from the past 12 weeks. It just means that you are not operating at your best, and that the probability of you hitting your goals is less than if you were executing at or above 80%.

4. Don't be afraid to confront what your numbers are telling you. If you are unwilling to confront reality, then you will never be able to change it.

THE FOUR WEEKLY EXECUTION SCENARIOS

If you score your execution each week, and you track your weekly lead and lag metrics for each of your goals, the 12 Week Year provides you with everything that you need to get better each week. Your weekly number will create one of four different scoring scenarios:

Scenario 1: You execute 80% or more of your tactics (+) and your lead and lag metrics are on track (+) to hit your 12 week goal.

Scenario 2: You execute less than 80% of your tactics (+) and your lead and lag metrics are *not* on track (–) to hit your 12 week goal.

Scenario 3: You execute 80% or more of your tactics (+) and your lead and lag metrics are *not* on track (–) to hit your 12 week goal.

Scenario 4: You execute less than 80% of your tactics (–) and your lead and lag metrics *are* on track (+) to hit your 12 week goal.

WEEKLY SCORE	LEAD & LAG MEASUREMENT
+	**+**
–	**–**
+	**–**
–	**+**

Measurement allows you to stay on track and focus on your most important activities each day of your 12 Week Year. Each of the scenarios above require you to take different actions to maximize the likelihood of hitting your 12 week goals. The following sections provide more details about each scenario.

Scenario 1 (++)

You are executing the tactics in your plan (80% +) and your plan tactics are working (your lead and lags are on pace to hit your goal.) This is the scenario you want every week. If you are in this situation in week 12, it means that you have hit your goals and have had a great 12 weeks! When you are scoring well and are on track to hit your 12 week goal, the actions for the upcoming week are simply to keep executing!

It is important to not get complacent in this scenario. Sometimes you can start to coast when things are going well. You get comfortable, take your foot off the gas, and your momentum stops. It is harder to get back up to speed after you slow down than it is to keep up a steady productive pace.

Scenario 2 (– –)

This scenario can be frustrating and even a bit demoralizing. You had the best of intentions, yet you just are not executing the tactics in your plan at a level that drives the results you are shooting for.

Often the first inclination in this scenario is to change your plan. But that is the wrong answer! You don't know if your plan works yet, because you are not working the plan.

The second common temptation in this scenario is to abandon your plan and the 12 Week Year with it, because, after all, you weren't doing *so* badly before. This is the worst approach. It is the only action that will guarantee your failure to hit your 12 week goals.

Instead, review the performance breakdown and what to do about it—the focus here is on your tactical execution. Once you ID the tactic, or tactics, that are not executing or avoiding, recommit to executing those tactics this week and to scoring 80%.

Here are some questions that may help you:

- Are there one or two tactics that you are avoiding?
- Do you keep your written weekly plan with you all the time and do you check in with it several times each day?
- Do you plan each day at the beginning of the day?
- If tactics are not done each day, do you stay or go home?
- What are you doing rather than working your plan?

Scenario 3 (+ –)

If you are executing at 80% or more but not moving your lead and lag measures at the pace needed to hit your 12 week goals, you are in an excellent position to get better results quickly. The hard part of the weekly execution process is usually scoring well on your tactics. To score well most often requires work and a willingness to be uncomfortable. Your weekly score shows that you are willing to work your plan, but your plan isn't working.

If you are not inflating your score, your lead metrics have had sufficient time to respond, and you are not consistently avoiding a specific tactic, the required action is to modify your plan so that when you execute it going forward, it delivers the results that you are expecting. Perhaps you need to increase activity, perhaps you need to refine your technique so that your process is more productive (add tactics to work on your sales talk, change up your work-out, carve out more time for coaching, and so on.)

The 12 Week Year is a learning system. And as adults we learn by iteration (trial and error.) You set a 12 week goal, you built a plan that you thought would work, and you executed it. Your results are less than what you need, so back to the plan you go!

If you change your plan, one of two things will happen: your changes will bear fruit and you will begin making sufficient progress on your goal, or you still are not seeing sufficient progress on your lead and lags. If you are making sufficient progress, great! If not, keep tweaking your plan until it delivers. This requires a willingness to work through the problem, but if you don't give up, you will reach a breakthrough moment. The only failure is giving up.

Scenario 4 (− +)

This is an unusual situation. You aren't working your plan (unless you are being too hard on yourself when you score,) but you are still hitting your goals.

Generally, there is one of three reasons for this outcome. The first is you got lucky. Something happened and all, or most, of your results just fell in your lap. Maybe you closed the deal of a lifetime. Maybe someone just showed up and bought all of your inventory, maybe the market is up. In any event, we recommend that you either raise your goal to reflect the lucky event, or mentally take it out of your results so that you are still executing your plan. While luck is great and feels good, it's not a process, and if you rely on it you are taking a huge risk of future failure.

The second reason that this scenario can happen is that your plan is much more difficult than necessary to hit your 12 week goal, but executing it at less than 80% is enough to hit your goal. In this case we recommend that you adjust your plan to make it more in line with what it takes to hit your goal, so that you don't run the risk of becoming demoralized.

The third common reason that scenario 4 arises is that you don't believe in your plan at all, and you are doing something else entirely that is driving your results. In this case we recommend that you replace the tactics in your plan with your new tactics. In this way, you set yourself up to be even more successful because a written plan is more productive than a plan between your ears, and you can keep tweaking your plan to make it even more effective.

———

GREAT WEEK AFTER GREAT WEEK: THE WEEKLY EXECUTION ROUTINE

Now that we have worked through Process Control and Scorekeeping, as promised earlier, we will explain what we call the Weekly Execution Routine, or WER. The WER is a three-step process that combines elements of Process Control and Scorekeeping and that if applied and fully engaged with, will almost guarantee that you will hit your 12 week goal!

Your 12 Week Year Plan schedules your tactics to come due a given week—not in a given day. This is because it generally does not matter if you get a tactic done on a Friday instead of a Tuesday. Rather, the problem arises when you let tactics slip from one week to the next. If that happens too much, you simply are setting yourself up to fail. That's why the week is the crucible for execution in the 12 Week Year. The WER keeps you on track and moving toward your goals every week.

WER Step 1—Score Last Week

At the end of each week, (or first thing Monday morning) score your week's execution and update your lead and lag metrics for each of your goals to reflect your results. It's best to do this before you begin the new week.

WEEKLY SCORECARD
Tactics completed / Total Tactics × 100 = your percentage   ☐ ÷ ☐ × 100 = ☐

Scoring will help you to prepare for the Weekly Accountability Meeting (WAM) (see Step 3 below) and to assess areas to focus on in the upcoming week. Maybe there was a breakdown to fix, maybe there was a success to celebrate. Maybe you need to catch up, maybe you need to score better this week, maybe you just need to keep going.

Scoring is sometimes a challenge because it's hard to confront performance breakdowns, but remember that if you can't measure it you can't manage it. Scoring not only supports effective execution, it also lets you focus on what's working and what needs to be improved.

A tip here is to prepare a summary of your results so that you are ready to be efficient with your time in the WAM. Another suggestion is to identify successes from the previous week.

WER Step 2—Write Down or Print Your Weekly Plan

Once you have completed scoring the previous week, it's time to create your new plan for the current week. If you are using our online tools on Achieve!, you will score your previous week and print your plan for the coming week. If you are using the paper system, you will create a weekly plan derived from your 12 Week Plan, and include all the tactics due this week plus any undone tactics from last week that must be made up in the current week to hit your 12 week goals. If you have weekly commitments you will include those in your weekly plan as well.

WER Step 3—Attend a WAM

Bring your plan and scores to the WAM and be prepared to report out as the CEO of your business and your life. Be sure to include successes, lessons learned, scores, and what is in your plan this week. If you need to execute better this week, let your WAM partners know exactly what you are committed to doing this week to get back on track. If you had any commitments that you made in last week's WAM, be sure to update the group on your progress.

Credit: Monkey Business Images/Shutterstock.com.

These three steps of the weekly execution routine are simple and easy. However, it is even simpler and easier not to do them. Commit to applying each of these tools every week this 12 Week Year and you will be amazed at the results.

The WER helps you to execute your plan consistently each week of the 12 Week Year. For an even deeper dive into your weekly execution, review Section 12 of this field guide.

CHAPTER 6

Using Your Time Intentionally

What if you were consistently able to get more of the important things done in your life and in your business every day? What would be different? Where could you be three months from now, three years from now?

Performance Time, our unique time-blocking system, will help you to allocate time to what matters most. Within just one week of applying the concepts, you will begin to see results, and you may feel more in control of your time than you have in years.

Performance Time is one of the five disciplines of the 12 Week Year. Combined with the other four—Vision, Planning, Process Control, and Scorekeeping—it is part of a proven execution system.

Everything that we achieve in life happens in the context of time. The important things will get done when we spend time on them. One of the building blocks of success is the ability to spend time on what matters most. Yet, we often hear our clients say something like, "I don't have time for the strategic. I'm just too busy!" Consciously they're thinking, "I want to do what I know is important," but their actions are saying, "My time is controlled by others and by outside events." People who are unwilling to change their actions will struggle to achieve their visions.

CONSTRUCTIVE BELIEF #1: YOUR TIME IS AT LEAST AS VALUABLE AS THE TIME OF OTHERS

Given the value, and the limited supply of time, it is interesting that almost all of us have difficulty spending it as effectively as we would like to. Many entrepreneurial clients we work with, driven by the natural desire to earn revenue whenever the opportunity arises,

Get your free resources at www.12weekyear.com/fieldguide

will discard their preplanned schedule without a second thought to accommodate the requests of prospects and clients. They do this repeatedly, seemingly without regard to the long-term impact on their business. In effect, the time that could be spent building their future is, instead, spent on building someone else's. We see similar behavior with our other clients as well—letting emergent opportunities or the requests of others pull them away from their preplanned activity.

In the final analysis, many of our clients value the time of others above their own. To achieve breakthrough, you must come to see your own time as at least as important as that of your clients. Only in this way can you build your business and, ironically, improve your client service at the same time.

___

CONSTRUCTIVE BELIEF #2: YOU CAN'T GET EVERYTHING DONE

One of the things that can get in the way of effective execution is the belief that we can get it all done. If we assume that if we work fast enough, hard enough, or long enough, we can do everything, then we are not required to prioritize our activity. Unfortunately, this is just not true. A recent study found that the average professional in America has more than 40 hours of unfinished work on his or her desk at any given time! That means that, no matter how hard we work, *we will never get it all done.*

Unless we realize the simple truth that we can't do it all, we will continue to labor under the false belief that we will eventually catch up, and "finally" get to that important stuff. We will continue to use all of our time on urgent day-to-day activities and postpone the strategic, but less urgent, work required to create a business breakthrough and, ultimately, the life we desire.

___

CONSTRUCTIVE BELIEF #3: WORK ON THE HIGH PRIORITY, MONEY-MAKING, RESULTS-GENERATING ACTIVITY FIRST

"You can change the future by what you do right now."

If you frequently defer your strategic work to accomplish the urgent, but lower-value activities, you will need a way to carve out time each week to work on your highest priority activity. If you work under the belief that you can eventually get the important things done by first working through the urgent, you will likely never get to the strategic stuff. The thinking that says, "I will start building my ideal future tomorrow, or next week, or next month," is flawed. The future you are going to live is the one you are creating right now—this very moment.

―――――

CONSTRUCTIVE BELIEF #4: BREAKTHROUGH REQUIRES BREAKOUT FROM YOUR OLD "SYSTEMS"

"If you're in control of your time, then you're in control of your results."

Reaching breakthrough isn't about being incremental. Breakthrough requires a profound change in the way that you work—before it shows up in your results. For some, breakthrough results may mean a 20% increase in income, or getting that promotion. For others, it may mean doubling their business. For still others, breakthrough may be taking more time off and continuing to increase their revenue. In each case, creating a breakthrough will require them to be willing to change how they spend their time.

These kinds of performance increases may sound inspiring, and yet, if you are already nearing the capacity of your current systems, you may honestly feel that there just isn't enough time in the week for "breakthrough."

Our clients often view higher performance levels as possible for others, but not possible for themselves. Many times, they feel that they are already working too hard, and the thought of working harder to earn more is unattractive. They may even have a real fear of success—the fear that says, "My current system cannot handle the level of activity that will come with greater success."

It feels like common sense to us that we have to work proportionally harder to earn more. Yet, that kind of thinking is exactly what limits what we can accomplish in life.

―――――

CONSTRUCTIVE ACTION: CREATE A MODEL WORKWEEK AND IMPLEMENT IT

The good news is that our clients earning $1,000,000 per year don't work 10 times harder than clients earning $100,000. In fact, sometimes they are working less! How is that possible?

You probably know, or have heard of, others who have overcome the breakthrough barrier of their own systems and thinking. They have solved the time "issue"; they have found a new way of working that increases their capacity to get the important things done. Unfortunately, there is a big difference between knowing that someone else can do it, and actually changing how we manage our time each day.

The fact is, that you won't reach a breakthrough if you don't change what you are currently doing with your time.

"To get different results, you will have to do things differently, and do different things."

After we take the important first step and make the commitment to spend our time on the important stuff, we next must know how to do it. Anytime we start to take new actions, it is helpful if we can visualize what the new actions look like. In the case of time allocation, we will have to create a picture of what the new time allocation looks like; we will have to create some version of a *Model Workweek*.

Performance Time is the breakthrough time-blocking system we have developed working with our clients. It allows you to operate like the CEO of your business and life by being intentional about how you spend your most valuable asset—your time. The commitment and ability to apply Performance Time is a manifestation of personal leadership. If you live with the intentionality of effective time use, you will become a more effective leader of those around you, and you will build your business and personal success at a faster rate.

There are three components that comprise a model workweek: *Strategic Blocks*, *Breakout Blocks*, and *Buffer Blocks*. Each of these three time blocks is designed to help you accomplish key activities more efficiently. In addition to these three categories, you will also want to schedule blocks of time to execute additional, important, recurring activities. Let's take a closer look at each type of block.

Strategic Blocks are three-hour blocks of time scheduled at least once a week. To be effective, strategic blocks should be conducted in one three-hour block (rather than three one-hour blocks) *and should be free from interruptions, such as: making or answering phone calls, answering knocks on your door, or responding to emails.*

An effective Strategic Block is focused on your *most important activities* that require uninterrupted time. A typical agenda in a strategic block might be to: (1) review your progress in the 12 Week Year, identify any performance breakdowns and their causes, and determine strategies to address the breakdowns; or (2) work on key plan tactics. We have found that Strategic Blocks are one of the top three contributors to success in applying the 12 Week Year effectively.

Your Strategic Block should be scheduled early in the week so that, if it gets interrupted or canceled, you have time to reschedule it. It should also be scheduled during times when your work activity is typically lowest.

Jot down some strategically important things that you might do in your Strategic Block (don't forget your strategic tactics from your 12 Week Plan):

Strategic Block Activities

Review Plan.

Review budget

Creative ideas.

Marketing research

_____

_____

_____

Buffer Blocks are 30–60 minutes in length and are scheduled once or twice a day—generally at the same time each day. They are designed to help you get all of the urgent, but less important stuff done more efficiently and effectively. The actual amount of time for buffer blocks will depend upon the amount of email, phone calls, interruptions, and other "administrivia" you typically are required to handle.

In these blocks of time, you will respond to emails, conduct short meetings, and answer your voice mail. (In fact, we recommend that you put a message on your system that says something like, "I am not available right now, but I typically return calls between 11 and 12, so please leave a message—I'll get back to you then.")

Buffer Blocks allow you to be more productive with the administrative tasks, and to free your more important time from interruptions that lower your effectiveness.

Take a few minutes and think through the low-value actions that are part of your workweek that might be included in your buffer blocks:

Buffer Block Activities

Budgets
_____
Admin
_____
Business / website
_____
Emails.
_____

_____

_____

_____

Breakout Blocks are also three hours in length. They are scheduled within your normal workweek, and are like a mini-vacation. In a Breakout Block, you get out of the office to do something that you enjoy. The only rule is that you don't do, or discuss, work. You may leave at noon on Thursday and golf. You may take your spouse to a long lunch. You may see a movie—it's up to you!

A Breakout Block is a chance for you to _recharge and refresh_—and to come back to work energized. They are an important part of managing stress and maintaining a balance at work.

One word of caution though—get the other aspects of the Model Workweek in place first. No one that we know has made it to the next level just by scheduling Breakout Blocks!

We recommend that you only have one per month until everything else is working and you are executing well.

Take a minute to capture some activities that would help you to get away and recharge.

Breakout Block Activities

3ws – manage
      movie
         dinner out.

_____

_____

_____

To implement performance time, using the blank weekly calendar template below, build an ideal week by scheduling your Strategic Blocks, Buffer Blocks, and Breakout Blocks where you would ideally like them (this is your "model" workweek).

How you choose to use your time has a direct impact on your results, both professionally and personally. Everything happens in the context of time and, if you are not in control of your time, then you are not in control of your results. Take back control of your day. Decide to apply Performance Time and achieve breakthrough in your business and your life.

Below, you will find the blank Model Workweek Table for you to schedule the performance time blocks and your other regularly standing commitments. Pencil in your blocks beginning with your Strategic Blocks, next moving to your Buffer Blocks, and then ending with your Breakout Block. Then fill in the other important activities that need to happen each week. Be sure to leave white space in your calendar, and to include time for executing your tactics that are not included in your Strategic Block (see the sample Model Weekly Timeblocking Template in Figure 6.1, found below the Model Week.)

Model Week

	Sunday	Monday	Tuesday	Wednesday	Thursday	Friday	Saturday
7 a.m.							
8 a.m.		Butter	Butter	Butter	Butter	Butter	
9 a.m.		Strategic					
10 a.m.							
11 a.m.		Strategic					
12 p.m.							
1 p.m.							
2 p.m.							
3 p.m.							
4 p.m.		Butter	Butter	Butter	Butter	Butter	Breakout
5 p.m.							
6 p.m.							
7 p.m.							

	Sunday	Monday	Tuesday	Wed.	Thursday	Friday	Saturday
7:00 am		Weekly Plan & Sc.	Buffer Block				
8:00 am		WAM		Appointment	Prospecting	Admin	
9:00 am			Strategic Block	Appointment			
10:00 am		Prospecting		Prospecting			
11:00 am		Buffer Block			Buffer Block		
12:00 pm			Referral Lunch	Buffer Block			
1:00 pm		Appointment	Appointment	Referral Lunch	Appointment		
2:00 pm		Appointment		Appointment	Appointment	Breakout Block 2nd and 4th Weeks	
3:00 pm					Appointment		
4:00 pm			Buffer Block				
5:00 pm							
6:00 pm							
7:00 pm							

Figure 6.1 Sample weekly time block

"This time, like all times, is a very good one, if we but know what to do with it."

— Ralph Waldo Emerson

Notice that the WAM, and the time to score and print the weekly plan, are included on Monday. It is important to score and plan after one week ends and before the next begins. Also note the five minutes at the beginning of each day to check in on their vision and plan the day.

It also helps to schedule your strategic block at a time of the week when you typically have the least activity or interruptions. When you schedule your strategic block earlier in the week, if it gets interrupted you can reschedule it in the same week. Consistency from day to day is also good—routine and patterns allow for easier coordination with others in your team.

COMMON PITFALLS

Do your best to avoid these four common pitfalls.

Pitfall 1: Not Being Willing to Change

The biggest obstacle our clients face in being more effective with their time is that they are just not willing to change. Over two-thirds of those attending our Live Event Workshops say they want to use their time more effectively. Yet, a significant percentage of those same people will not do anything differently. Structuring your time differently creates a considerable amount of discomfort. That is not necessarily good or bad. Change is uncomfortable. That's just the way it is—get over it! If you want things you don't currently have, you will have to do things you're not currently doing. If you want to perform at your best, you will need to be more effective with how you use your time.

Pitfall 2: Finding Reasons Why It Won't Work

In every workshop I conduct, there are always a number of people who will passionately tell me why the time blocking concept won't work for them. They have convinced them-selves that it won't work before they have even tried the concept. That is like deciding that you don't like a particular food without ever having tasted it. Henry Ford said, "If you think you can, or you think you can't, you're right!"

Pitfall 3: Not Sticking with It

Changing the way that you use your time is difficult and sometimes painful. Don't make the mistake of quitting before you've mastered the concept. Developing new habits and rou-tines takes time. Everything in your being will want to revert back to what is familiar and comfortable. Stick with it. Take ownership and make the concepts work for you. Make a commitment to apply the system.

Pitfall 4: Compromising the Time Blocks

As people begin time blocking, the tendency is to revert back to the old familiar ways, and so they will often compromise their blocks, especially the Strategic Block. Don't do it! Keep your Strategic Block sacred. Use it only for strategic activity, and don't schedule over it. In the rare event where an emergency arises that forces you to abandon your Strategic Block, reschedule it. Get it back on the calendar for later that day, or later that week.

CHAPTER 7

---

12 Week Year Review and Planning

What do you do at the end of your 12 Week Year? Keep going! You have spent a considerable amount of time and effort to install the 12 Week Year. Don't waste your investment. Take some time to capture the lessons learned and to set up your next 12 Week plan.

When you have finished a 12 Week Year, it's time to celebrate success, capture learning, and to launch again. The 12 Week Year execution cycle is a powerful process that enables you to align your actions with your intentions and actualize the best you possible. This chapter will take you through a robust review of the past 12 weeks—the good, the bad, and the ugly. It is structured to provide valuable insight and promote learning that you can build off of in the next 12 weeks.

To become great, to attain breakthrough, takes execution—not a new idea. Great ideas are worthless unless they get executed. That's what the 12 Week Year is—it is a system that helps you to execute effectively.

Michael Phelps wasn't great because he knew a secret training technique—most top swimmers have access to great trainers—instead, he was great when he ate the right foods, swam the laps, and *executed* his training plan. All the Olympic medals he won were the evidence of his greatness at executing.

The 12 Week Year isn't about a new idea for marketing or losing weight, the 12 Week Year is a system that shifts the way that you think and act and helps you to take action on the things you need to do to be great—to execute well. But it is more than just an execution system—it is also a learning system. Every 12 weeks it is designed to capture your learning and to build that learning into your next 12 Week Year Plan.

To effectively capture learning from your past 12 Week Year, schedule a two-hour block of time where you can focus without distractions. Before working through the

Get your free resources at www.12weekyear.com/fieldguide

sections below, gather your plan from the most recent 12 Week Year, and your weekly plans and scorecards. Once you have collected what you need and have carved out sufficient time, complete the following 12 Week Year review and planning sections.

---

12 WEEK YEAR REVIEW AND PLANNING

To begin, we will have you complete a comprehensive review of the 12 Week Year you just finished. An extensive and honest look into your results will be helpful in determining what was effective as well as areas where you can improve.

Results and Execution

Measurement is the link with reality that tells you how you are doing—how your actions are impacting the world. Metrics provide you with important information you need to make intelligent and productive decisions. In this first section of the review, you will document your results and your execution.

12 WEEK GOALS		1	2	3	4	5	6	7	8	9	10	
GOAL #1	No Real Progress on Goal											Accomplished Goal
GOALS #2	No Real Progress on Goal											Accomplished Goal
GOALS #3	No Real Progress on Goal											Accomplished Goal

EXECUTION						
SCORES	WK1	WK2	WK3	WK4	WK5	WK6
12 Week Average ____	____	____	____	____	____	____
	WK7	WK8	WK9	WK10	WK11	WK12
	____	____	____	____	____	____

For each goal, mark the percentage of achievement. As an example, if you accomplished 100% of your first goal, then you would check the box for 10. If you only accomplished about half of your goal then you would check 5. Next, review your weekly scores (do this by goal if you have that information—if you don't, use your overall weekly score.)

Looking at your results and your execution, what insights can you draw—what worked, and what didn't?

_____

_____

_____

_____

_____

_____

_____

_____

Did you average 80% or better on your Weekly Plan & Scorecard? If not, what do you need to do differently to achieve this standard?

_____

_____

_____

_____

_____

_____

_____

_____

_____

_____

QUALITY OF LIFE

The concept of life balance is an illusion. We're led to believe that somehow we can spend equal time in all the various areas of life: family, work, spouse, health, friends, and community. That's just not possible. And even if it were, I doubt it would create the joy and fulfillment that it promises.

Rather than seek life balance, we recommend that you strive for intentional imbalance. There will be times in life—seasons if you will—when you decide to spend more time in one area over another. There is nothing wrong with that. The key is that it is intentional, and by design.

In this section, you will create a snapshot of six key life areas. As you complete this section, base your rating on your level of satisfaction in each area. Then identify the direction of movement with an arrow that points either left, if satisfaction is decreasing, or an arrow that points right if your satisfaction is on the rise.

QUALITY OF LIFE		1	2	3	4	5	6	7	8	9	10	
SPIRITUAL	Spiritually Empty, no Foundation											Living in alignment with beliefs
SPOUSE/KEY RELATIONSHIP	Relationship Strained, Unfulfilling											Relationship is Vibrant, Loving, & Full
FAMILY	Lack Quality Time, Don't Feel Close											Family Life is Full & Meaningful
BUSINESS	Not in Control Lack Direction, Feel Frustrated											Business is Thriving & Fulfilling
PERSONAL	No Time for Self, Not Growing, Stagnant											Taking Life On with Energy & Enthusiasm
PHYSICAL	Poor Physical Condition, Poor Health											Excellent Physical Condition, Excellent Health

What areas are you pleased with?

_____

_____

_____

_____

_____

_____

_____

What areas do you want to improve this next 12 weeks?

_____

_____

_____

_____

_____

_____

_____

_____

—————

SUCCESS DISCIPLINES

This next grid represents the fundamental disciplines of success. There are five success disciplines: Vision, Planning, Process Control, Scorekeeping, and Time Use. Learning to effectively leverage these disciplines will lead to greater and greater success. Rate your level of engagement with these disciplines over the past 12 weeks.

As you review your engagement with these disciplines, what insights emerge for you?

SUCCESS DISCIPLINES		1	2	3	4	5	6	7	8	9	10	
VISION	Lack connection with Vision											Clear connection between Vision & daily activity
12 WEEK PLANNING	Did not have/ use a 12 Week Plan											Created and used a 12 Week Plan
WEEKLY ROUTINE	Did not Plan, Score or WAM each Week											Used Weekly Plan, Scorecard & WAM
PERFORMANCE TIME	No Strategic, Break-Out, or Buffer Blocks											Effective use of Time Blocking System
KEY MEASURES	Not tracking critical measures											Effectively managing lead & lag indicators

What disciplines will you commit to leveraging more effectively this next 12 weeks?

_____

_____

_____

_____

_____

_____

_____

———

BREAKTHROUGHS

With the 12 Week Year, every 12 weeks is a fresh start, a new opportunity to learn from the past and apply that learning in a powerful way to accomplish even greater things. In this last section, we will have you take a look at what it will take to create a breakthrough in the next 12 weeks.

Describe your most significant accomplishment in the past 12 weeks:

_____

_____

_____

_____

_____

_____

_____

How would your thinking need to change in order for you to double the results you achieved these past 12 weeks?

What new actions will you need to take during these next 12 weeks for you to breakthrough?

When you have completed the 12 Week Year review and are ready to create your new 12 Week Year Plan, schedule a few hours in your calendar to work through the process. Don't wait to get started. This is your second 12 Week Year coming up—don't lose all the momentum that you have from your last 12 weeks—build on it instead!

CHAPTER 8

Confront the Truth
(Optional Section)

This section is optional, but then so is success!

Each week of your 12 Week Year is an opportunity to either move forward, or to lose ground. The choice is yours.

If you want to achieve your 12 week goals, it is vital that you learn to confront the truth about your performance each week. If you are scoring your week and you are tracking at least one lead and lag measure for each of your 12 week goals, you have what you need to get better every week and dramatically increase your odds of being successful with your 12 Week Year.

When you take ownership of your goal, that ownership is manifested in your actions. The first actions that indicate that you own your plan are: (1) consistently scoring your week, (2) working from a written weekly plan, and (3) attending a weekly accountability meeting—either in a WAM with your peers, with a coach, or with an accountability partner.

The next level of ownership is evidenced by how effectively you confront the truth. Specifically, you need to face the truth about your execution. Each week you have a choice: to do the work to get better, or to avoid discomfort and the work. It is that simple—and it is that hard.

Becoming great isn't an intellectual process. It isn't a complex process. In reality, it is an amazingly simple process. The path to becoming great is simply doing the work, and that is usually uncomfortable.

This is the reason why most people don't try to get better, and often why they stop using the 12 Week Year; *their comfort is more important to them than their success.*

Get your free resources at www.12weekyear.com/fieldguide

Don't let this describe you. Don't settle for less than you are capable of. If you are serious about your 12 week goal, and accomplishing what you are capable of, learn to *confront the truth* each week, and to take the actions that are necessary to reach your goals.

In the pages that follow are what you might call your weekly "confront the truth" worksheets. They combine your weekly score and the progress you are making toward your goals, and prompt you to take action to keep going or to get back on track. They will help you (and your accountability partners) to assess what you need to do—given where you are in your 12 Week Year. They will take about 10 to 20 minutes to work through, but if you use them, they will identify what actions are needed to execute well in the upcoming week.

If you find that you can't dedicate this amount of time each week, then consider using the tool to conduct a monthly progress review every four weeks.

To help you engage with the weekly confront-the-truth process, it will be helpful to see an example first.

CONFRONTING THE TRUTH EXAMPLE—12 WEEK EXECUTION DATA

Background

- This example assumes that it is Monday morning on week 7, and you are reviewing **week 6** execution results.
- Your 12 week goal is to "**Produce $12,000 in revenue**."
- Your lead measure that you are tracking for this goal: **Weekly meetings**.
- Your weekly target for your lead measure: **10 meetings per week** (120 meetings for the entire 12 Week Year).
- The lag measure that you are tracking for this goal: **Revenue**.
- The weekly target for your lag measure: **$1,000** ($12,000 for the 12WY)

See the sample worksheet below.

Sample Confront the Truth Worksheet

Weekly Execution Score

Last Week's Execution Score	Average Execution Score-to-Date
75%	55%

Weekly Lead and Lag Measures
Lead measures

Actual	Target
Last week: 8 meetings	Weekly target: 10 meetings
Week-six cumulative actual: 42 meetings	Week-six cumulative target: 60 meetings

Lag measures

Actual	Target
Production to Date: $4,000	Production Target to Date: $6,000

Week-to-Week Scoring and Lead/Lag Trends   *Scores started low but are getting better, I am using strategic blocks better than I was*

Risks/Issues/Gaps to Address   *Meetings are consistently low, will have to pick up activity. Need to ask for more referrals—do this at every close!!!*

Performance Breakdowns   *Not executing referral tactic consistently so no warm leads to call—I'm not following talk. I have to practice the talk more and ask!*

Action Commitment(s) for This Week   *Ask for referrals in every meeting—practice talk Tuesday 2–4 and Thursday 8–10 this week. Get feedback on my referral talk from my coach.*

━━━━━

CONFRONTING THE TRUTH

Now it's time for you to confront your own truth. When you prepare for this exercise you will need to gather the same information as shown in the example in the preceding section.

You will need your completed weekly plans for the 12 Week Year to date, your lead and lag measures for each week, and you will need to know your weekly target (the number you need to achieve each week to hit your 12 week goal) for each lead and lag measure you are tracking. For a PDF of the Confront The Truth worksheets, visit www.12weekyear.com/fieldguide.

Confront the Truth Worksheet: Week 1

Weekly Execution Score   *(If more than one goal, complete this section for each goal.)*

Last Week's Execution Score	Average Execution Score-to-Date

Weekly Lead and Lag Measures by Goal   *(If more than 1 lead or lag measure, complete for each measure)*

Lead Measure

Actual	Target
Last week:	Weekly target:
Week-one cumulative actual:	Week-one cumulative target:

Lag Measure

Actual	Target
Last week:	Weekly target:
Week-one cumulative actual:	Week-one cumulative target:

Week-to-Week Scoring and Lead/Lag Trends:

_____

_____

_____

_____

_____

_____

Risks/Issues/Gaps to Address:

_____

_____

_____

_____

_____

Performance Breakdowns: _(Be sure to ID any tactics you are avoiding.)_

_____

_____

_____

_____

Action Commitment(s) for This Week:

_____

_____

_____

_____

_____

Confront the Truth Worksheet: Week 2

Weekly Execution Score　　*(If more than one goal, complete this section for each goal.)*

Last Week's Execution Score	Average Execution Score-to-Date

Weekly Lead and Lag Measures by Goal　　*(If more than 1 lead or lag measure, complete for each measure)*

Lead Measure.

Actual	Target
Last week:	Weekly target:
Week-two cumulative actual:	Week-two cumulative target:

Lag Measure

Actual	Target
Last week:	Weekly target:
Week-two cumulative actual:	Week-two cumulative target:

Week-to-Week Scoring and Lead/Lag Trends:

_____

_____

_____

_____

_____

Risks/Issues/Gaps to Address:

_____

_____

_____

_____

_____

Performance Breakdowns: _(Be sure to ID any tactics you are avoiding.)_

_____

_____

_____

_____

_____

Action Commitment(s) for This Week:

_____

_____

_____

_____

_____

Confront the Truth Worksheet: Week 3

Weekly Execution Score   *(If more than one goal, complete this section for each goal.)*

Last Week's Execution Score	Average Execution Score-to-Date

Weekly Lead and Lag Measures by Goal   *(If more than 1 lead or lag measure, complete for each measure)*

Lead Measure

Actual	Target
Last week:	Weekly target:
Week-three cumulative actual:	Week-three cumulative target:

Lag Measure

Actual	Target
Last week:	Weekly target:
Week-three cumulative actual:	Week-three cumulative target:

Week-to-Week Scoring and Lead/Lag Trends:

_____

_____

_____

_____

_____

Risks/Issues/Gaps to Address:

_____

_____

_____

_____

_____

Performance Breakdowns: _(Be sure to ID any tactics you are avoiding.)_

_____

_____

_____

_____

_____

Action Commitment(s) for This Week:

_____

_____

_____

_____

_____

Confront the Truth Worksheet: Week 4

Weekly Execution Score   *(If more than one goal, complete this section for each goal.)*

Last Week's Execution Score	Average Execution Score-to-Date

Weekly Lead and Lag Measures by Goal   *(If more than 1 lead or lag measure, complete for each measure)*

Lead Measure

Actual	Target
Last week:	Weekly target:
Week-four cumulative actual:	Week-four cumulative target:

Lag Measure

Actual	Target
Last week:	Weekly target:
Week-four cumulative actual:	Week-four cumulative target:

Week-to-Week Scoring and Lead/Lag Trends:

_____

_____

_____

_____

_____

Risks/Issues/Gaps to Address:

_____

_____

_____

_____

_____

Performance Breakdowns: _(Be sure to ID any tactics you are avoiding.)_

_____

_____

_____

_____

_____

Action Commitment(s) for This Week:

_____

_____

_____

_____

_____

Confront the Truth Worksheet: Week 5

Weekly Execution Score   *(If more than one goal, complete this section for each goal.)*

Last Week's Execution Score	Average Execution Score-to-Date

Weekly Lead and Lag Measures by Goal   *(If more than 1 lead or lag measure, complete for each measure)*

Lead Measure

Actual	Target
Last week:	Weekly target:
Week-five cumulative actual:	Week-five cumulative target:

Lag Measure

Actual	Target
Last week:	Weekly target:
Week-five cumulative actual:	Week-five cumulative target:

Week-to-Week Scoring and Lead/Lag Trends:

_____

_____

_____

_____

_____

Risks/Issues/Gaps to Address:

_____

_____

_____

_____

_____

Performance Breakdowns: _(Be sure to ID any tactics you are avoiding.)_

_____

_____

_____

_____

Action Commitment(s) for This Week:

_____

_____

_____

_____

Confront the Truth Worksheet: Week 6

Weekly Execution Score   *(If more than one goal, complete this section for each goal.)*

Last Week's Execution Score	Average Execution Score-to-Date

Weekly Lead and Lag Measures by Goal   *(If more than 1 lead or lag measure, complete for each measure)*

Lead Measure

Actual	Target
Last week:	Weekly target:
Week-six cumulative actual:	Week-six cumulative target:

Lag Measure

Actual	Target
Last week:	Weekly target:
Week-six cumulative actual:	Week-six cumulative target:

Week-to-Week Scoring and Lead/Lag Trends:

_____

_____

_____

_____

_____

Risks/Issues/Gaps to Address:

_____

_____

_____

_____

_____

Performance Breakdowns: _(Be sure to ID any tactics you are avoiding.)_

_____

_____

_____

_____

_____

Action Commitment(s) for This Week:

_____

_____

_____

_____

_____

Confront the Truth Worksheet: Week 7

Weekly Execution Score *(If more than one goal, complete this section for each goal.)*

Last Week's Execution Score	Average Execution Score-to-Date

Weekly Lead and Lag Measures by Goal *(If more than 1 lead or lag measure, complete for each measure)*

Lead Measure

Actual	Target
Last week:	Weekly target:
Week-seven cumulative actual:	Week-seven cumulative target:

Lag Measure

Actual	Target
Last week:	Weekly target:
Week-seven cumulative actual:	Week-seven cumulative target:

Week-to-Week Scoring and Lead/Lag Trends:

_____

_____

_____

_____

_____

Risks/Issues/Gaps to Address:

_____

_____

_____

_____

_____

Performance Breakdowns: _(Be sure to ID any tactics you are avoiding.)_

_____

_____

_____

_____

_____

Action Commitment(s) for This Week:

_____

_____

_____

_____

_____

Confront the Truth Worksheet: Week 8

Weekly Execution Score   *(If more than one goal, complete this section for each goal.)*

Last Week's Execution Score	Average Execution Score-to-Date

Weekly Lead and Lag Measures by Goal   *(If more than 1 lead or lag measure, complete for each measure)*

Lead Measure

Actual	Target
Last week:	Weekly target:
Week-eight cumulative actual:	Week-eight cumulative target:

Lag Measure

Actual	Target
Last week:	Weekly target:
Week-eight cumulative actual:	Week-eight cumulative target:

Week-to-Week Scoring and Lead/Lag Trends:

_____

_____

_____

_____

_____

Risks/Issues/Gaps to Address:

_____

_____

_____

_____

_____

Performance Breakdowns: _(Be sure to ID any tactics you are avoiding.)_

_____

_____

_____

_____

_____

Action Commitment(s) for This Week:

_____

_____

_____

_____

_____

Confront the Truth Worksheet: Week 9

Weekly Execution Score   *(If more than one goal, complete this section for each goal.)*

Last Week's Execution Score	Average Execution Score-to-Date

Weekly Lead and Lag Measures by Goal   *(If more than 1 lead or lag measure, complete for each measure)*

Lead Measure

Actual	Target
Last week:	Weekly target:
Week-nine cumulative actual:	Week-nine cumulative target:

Lag Measure

Actual	Target
Last week:	Weekly target:
Week-nine cumulative actual:	Week-nine cumulative target:

Week-to-Week Scoring and Lead/Lag Trends:

_____

_____

_____

_____

_____

Risks/Issues/Gaps to Address:

_____

_____

_____

_____

_____

Performance Breakdowns: _(Be sure to ID any tactics you are avoiding.)_

_____

_____

_____

_____

_____

Action Commitment(s) for This Week:

_____

_____

_____

_____

_____

Confront the Truth Worksheet: Week 10

Weekly Execution Score   *(If more than one goal, complete this section for each goal.)*

Last Week's Execution Score	Average Execution Score-to-Date

Weekly Lead and Lag Measures by Goal   *(If more than 1 lead or lag measure, complete for each measure)*

Lead Measure

Actual	Target
Last week:	Weekly target:
Week-ten cumulative actual:	Week-ten cumulative target:

Lag Measure

Actual	Target
Last week:	Weekly target:
Week-ten cumulative actual:	Week-ten cumulative target:

Week-to-Week Scoring and Lead/Lag Trends:

_____

_____

_____

_____

_____

Risks/Issues/Gaps to Address:

_____

_____

_____

_____

_____

Performance Breakdowns: _(Be sure to ID any tactics you are avoiding.)_

_____

_____

_____

_____

_____

Action Commitment(s) for This Week:

_____

_____

_____

_____

_____

Confront the Truth Worksheet: Week 11

Weekly Execution Score   *(If more than one goal, complete this section for each goal.)*

Last Week's Execution Score	Average Execution Score-to-Date

Weekly Lead and Lag Measures by Goal   *(If more than 1 lead or lag measure, complete for each measure)*

Lead Measure

Actual	Target
Last week:	Weekly target:
Week-eleven cumulative actual:	Week-eleven cumulative target:

Lag Measure

Actual	Target
Last week:	Weekly target:
Week-eleven cumulative actual:	Week-eleven cumulative target:

Week-to-Week Scoring and Lead/Lag Trends:

_____

_____

_____

_____

_____

Risks/Issues/Gaps to Address:

_____

_____

_____

_____

_____

Performance Breakdowns: *(Be sure to ID any tactics you are avoiding.)*

_____

_____

_____

_____

_____

Action Commitment(s) for This Week:

_____

_____

_____

_____

_____

Confront the Truth Worksheet: Week 12

Weekly Execution Score   *(If more than one goal, complete this section for each goal.)*

Last Week's Execution Score	Average Execution Score-to-Date

Weekly Lead and Lag Measures by Goal   *(If more than 1 lead or lag measure, complete for each measure)*

Lead Measure

Actual	Target
Last week:	Weekly target:
Week-twelve cumulative actual:	Week-twelve cumulative target:

Lag Measure

Actual	Target
Last week:	Weekly target:
Week-twelve cumulative actual:	Week-twelve cumulative target:

Week-to-Week Scoring and Lead/Lag Trends:

_____

_____

_____

_____

_____

Risks/Issues/Gaps to Address:

_____

_____

_____

_____

_____

Performance Breakdowns: _(Be sure to ID any tactics you are avoiding.)_

_____

_____

_____

_____

_____

Action Commitment(s) for This Week:

_____

_____

_____

_____

_____

CHAPTER 9

---

12 Week Year Game Plan

This section includes a 12 Week planning template and 13 Weekly Plans. If you would like additional copies, please visit us at www.12weekyear.com/fieldguide and download the free PDF files available there.

At the beginning of your 12 Week Year, use the planning template to record your goals and the tactics needed to reach them. Be sure to include the week(s) that each tactic comes due.

At the beginning of each week, use a Weekly Plan to capture tactics due from your 12 Week Plan. If you have any past due tactics that are still relevant, include them in your Weekly Plan as well. Tactics that came due in earlier weeks, or that are not yet due, *are not* included in your Weekly Plan. Once your Weekly Plan is prepared, carry it with you and execute from it each day.

12 WEEK GOALS

GOALS
>
>
>

12 WEEK PLAN
GOAL #1:

KEY ACTIONS/TACTICS	WEEK DUE

GOAL #2:

KEY ACTIONS/TACTICS	WEEK DUE

GOAL #3:

KEY ACTIONS/TACTICS	WEEK DUE

GOAL #4:

KEY ACTIONS/TACTICS	WEEK DUE

GOAL #5:

KEY ACTIONS/TACTICS	WEEK DUE

GOAL #6:

KEY ACTIONS/TACTICS	WEEK DUE

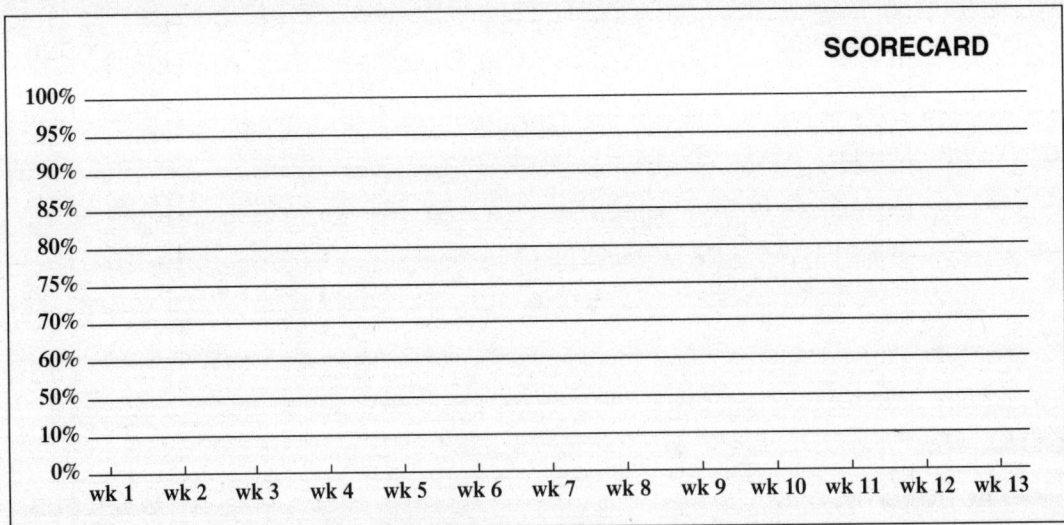

SCORECARD

100%
95%
90%
85%
80%
75%
70%
60%
50%
10%
0%

wk 1   wk 2   wk 3   wk 4   wk 5   wk 6   wk 7   wk 8   wk 9   wk 10   wk 11   wk 12   wk 13

WEEKLY PLAN & SCORECARD

Week 1

12 WEEK GOAL: _____

_____

KEY ACTIONS/TACTICS List of your key actions and the day you wish to complete them	WHO	DAY

TIME BLOCK Set up your time blocks for the week	DAY/TIME
Strategic block	
Buffer blocks	

" *An aspiration or desire means little without a plan to get there* "
      – Unknown

WEEKLY SCORECARD Tactics Completed / Total Tactics X 100 = your percentage	☐ ÷ ☐ X 100 = ☐ %

THE 12 WEEK YEAR

Get your free resources at www.12weekyear.com/fieldguide

WEEKLY PLAN & SCORECARD

Week 2

12 WEEK GOAL: _____

_____

KEY ACTIONS/TACTICS List of your key actions and the day you wish to complete them	WHO	DAY

TIME BLOCK Set up your time blocks for the week	DAY/TIME
Strategic block	
Buffer blocks	

"An aspiration or desire means little without a plan to get there"
— Unknown

THE 12 WEEK YEAR

WEEKLY SCORECARD Tactics Completed / Total Tactics X 100 = your percentage	☐ ÷ ☐ x 100 = ☐ %

Get your free resources at www.12weekyear.com/fieldguide

WEEKLY PLAN & SCORECARD

Week 3

12 WEEK GOAL:

KEY ACTIONS/TACTICS List of your key actions and the day you wish to complete them	WHO	DAY

TIME BLOCK Set up your time blocks for the week	DAY/TIME
Strategic block	
Buffer blocks	

"An aspiration or desire means little without a plan to get there"

— Unknown

THE 12 WEEK YEAR

WEEKLY SCORECARD Tactics Completed / Total Tactics X 100 = your percentage	☐ ÷ ☐ x 100 = ☐ %

WEEKLY PLAN & SCORECARD

Week 4

12 WEEK GOAL: _____

_____

KEY ACTIONS/TACTICS List of your key actions and the day you wish to complete them	WHO	DAY

TIME BLOCK Set up your time blocks for the week	DAY/TIME
Strategic block	
Buffer blocks	

" An aspiration or desire means little without a plan to get there"

- Unknown

THE 12 WEEK YEAR

WEEKLY SCORECARD Tactics Completed / Total Tactics X 100 = your percentage	☐ ÷ ☐ x 100 = ☐ %

Get your free resources at www.12weekyear.com/fieldguide

WEEKLY PLAN & SCORECARD

Week 5

12 WEEK GOAL: _____

_____

KEY ACTIONS/TACTICS List of your key actions and the day you wish to complete them	WHO	DAY

TIME BLOCK Set up your time blocks for the week	DAY/TIME
Strategic block	
Buffer blocks	

" An aspiration or desire means little without a plan to get there"
— Unknown

THE 12 WEEK YEAR

WEEKLY SCORECARD Tactics Completed / Total Tactics X 100 = your percentage	☐ ÷ ☐ x 100 = ☐ %

WEEKLY PLAN & SCORECARD

Week 6

12 WEEK GOAL: _____

_____

KEY ACTIONS/TACTICS List of your key actions and the day you wish to complete them	WHO	DAY

TIME BLOCK Set up your time blocks for the week	DAY/TIME
Strategic block	
Buffer blocks	

"An aspiration or desire means little without a plan to get there"

– Unknown

WEEKLY SCORECARD
Tactics Completed / Total Tactics X 100 = your percentage

[ ] ÷ [ ] x 100 = [ ] %

THE 12 WEEK YEAR

WEEKLY PLAN & SCORECARD

Week 7

12 WEEK GOAL: _____

_____

KEY ACTIONS/TACTICS List of your key actions and the day you wish to complete them	WHO	DAY

TIME BLOCK Set up your time blocks for the week	DAY/TIME
Strategic block	
Buffer blocks	

"An aspiration or desire means little without a plan to get there"
— Unknown

THE 12 WEEK YEAR

WEEKLY SCORECARD Tactics Completed / Total Tactics X 100 = your percentage	☐ ÷ ☐ x 100 = ☐ %

WEEKLY PLAN & SCORECARD

Week 8

12 WEEK GOAL:

KEY ACTIONS/TACTICS List of your key actions and the day you wish to complete them	WHO	DAY

TIME BLOCK Set up your time blocks for the week	DAY/TIME
Strategic block	
Buffer blocks	

" An aspiration or desire means little without a plan to get there"

– Unknown

WEEKLY SCORECARD
Tactics Completed / Total Tactics X 100 = your percentage

☐ ÷ ☐ x 100 = ☐ %

THE 12 WEEK YEAR

WEEKLY PLAN & SCORECARD

Week 9

12 WEEK GOAL: _____

_____

KEY ACTIONS/TACTICS List of your key actions and the day you wish to complete them	WHO	DAY

TIME BLOCK Set up your time blocks for the week	DAY/TIME
Strategic block	
Buffer blocks	

" An aspiration or desire means little without a plan to get there"
– Unknown

THE 12 WEEK YEAR

WEEKLY SCORECARD Tactics Completed / Total Tactics X 100 = your percentage	☐ ÷ ☐ x 100 = ☐ %

WEEKLY PLAN & SCORECARD

Week 10

12 WEEK GOAL: _____

KEY ACTIONS/TACTICS List of your key actions and the day you wish to complete them	WHO	DAY

TIME BLOCK Set up your time blocks for the week	DAY/TIME
Strategic block	
Buffer blocks	

"An aspiration or desire means little without a plan to get there"
- Unknown

THE 12 WEEK YEAR

WEEKLY SCORECARD Tactics Completed / Total Tactics X 100 = your percentage	☐ ÷ ☐ x 100 = ☐ %

Get your free resources at www.12weekyear.com/fieldguide

WEEKLY PLAN & SCORECARD

Week 11

12 WEEK GOAL: _____

_____

KEY ACTIONS/TACTICS List of your key actions and the day you wish to complete them	WHO	DAY

TIME BLOCK Set up your time blocks for the week	DAY/TIME
Strategic block	
Buffer blocks	

" An aspiration or desire means little without a plan to get there"
– Unknown

THE
12
WEEK
YEAR

WEEKLY SCORECARD Tactics Completed / Total Tactics X 100 = your percentage	☐ ÷ ☐ x 100 = ☐ %

Get your free resources at www.12weekyear.com/fieldguide

WEEKLY PLAN & SCORECARD

Week 12

12 WEEK GOAL: _____

_____

KEY ACTIONS/TACTICS List of your key actions and the day you wish to complete them	WHO	DAY

TIME BLOCK Set up your time blocks for the week	DAY/TIME
Strategic block	
Buffer blocks	

" An aspiration or desire means little without a plan to get there"

– Unknown

THE 12 WEEK YEAR

WEEKLY SCORECARD Tactics Completed / Total Tactics X 100 = your percentage	☐ ÷ ☐ x 100 = ☐ %

WEEKLY PLAN & SCORECARD

Week 13 ⏳

12 WEEK GOAL:

KEY ACTIONS/TACTICS List of your key actions and the day you wish to complete them	WHO	DAY

TIME BLOCK Set up your time blocks for the week	DAY/TIME
Strategic block	
Buffer blocks	

"An aspiration or desire means little without a plan to get there"
– Unknown

WEEKLY SCORECARD
Tactics Completed / Total Tactics X 100 = your percentage   ☐ ÷ ☐ x 100 = ☐ %

THE 12 WEEK YEAR

CONCLUSION

That's it! If you've gotten this far, you are officially ready to execute with the 12 Week Year! Congratulations and welcome to the growing community of 12 Week Year practitioners. Now, the good stuff happens.

You have a vision and 12 week goals. You have a 12 Week Action Plan to reach those goals. You have the Weekly Plan templates to keep you on track each and every week of the 12 Week Year.

All that's left is for you to immerse yourself in the energy and focus of the system. Don't start a week without a plan. Don't end a week without scoring. Have the courage to confront your performance breakdowns and learn from them.

Thomas Edison said that if we only did what we are capable of doing, we would astound ourselves. You are capable of great things! You have everything you need to be great *right now*. Stop waiting to be great and start acting – create your first weekly plan and start executing it. In a very short time, you will be amazed at the changes in your thinking, actions, and results.

Have an astounding 12 weeks!

ABOUT THE AUTHORS

 **BRIAN MORAN** is the driving force behind many of the successful entrepreneurs and leaders in industry today. His unique combination of experience and insight provides a platform for individuals and organizations to take quantum leaps in their performance. Brian's breakthrough approach has been field tested and proven.

As a speaker, Brian is thought provoking and passionate. He challenges the audience with action based concepts and strategies. His engaging and interactive sessions range from a one-hour keynote to a two-day workshop. Whatever the length, the sessions challenge the "business as usual" mentality and offer fresh insights into what it takes to achieve greatness. Participants leave inspired to take action and committed to greater possibilities.

Partial client list: AXA, Allstate, BBVA Compass, Becton Dickinson, Mass Mutual, MDRT, Medtronic, Merrill Lynch, Nationwide, New York Life, Northwestern Mutual, Papa Johns, and State Farm, to name a few.

MICHAEL LENNINGTON, coauthor of *The 12 Week Year*, works with firms and top performers to help them create next-level breakthroughs by leveraging the 12 Week Year execution system.

For individuals and teams who are already successful, but have hit the limits of their current systems, Michael helps his clients to double, triple, and even quadruple their results without just "working harder" through his guided approach to applying the 12 Week Year.

Join the conversation!

CONNECT WITH US TODAY FOR 12 WEEK YEAR NEWS AND FREE EXECUTION CONTENT.

 "Like" us on Facebook: The 12 Week Year

LinkedIn: Brian P. Moran, Michael Lennington

 Follow us on Twitter: @brianpmoran, @MLennington

 Pin us on Pinterest: 12 Week Year

MAXIMIZE
your 12 Week Year results
with the power of a
COACH!

Ensure your success with hands-on support that virtually guarantees your results!

Small Group Coaching
Take advantage of the powerful combination of customized Coaching and peer support to raise your execution quotient and achieve your capability.

One-On-One Coaching
Work one-on-one with your Certified 12 Week Year Coach to ensure that you leverage the 12 Week Year System and crush your goals.

SERVICES

SPEAKING & IN-HOUSE TRAINING

Brian P. Moran is available to speak directly to your team. Brian will show your team what it takes to execute at a high level and achieve their goals and aspirations in just 12 short weeks. Brian's engaging and interactive sessions include a 1-hour keynote, half-day and full-day workshop, and offer fresh insight into what it takes to achieve greatness.

COACHING

The 12 Week Year offers one-on-one and small group coaching that gets results. Our coaching helps you to get up to speed on the 12 Week Year quickly and with greatest impact. Your 12 week coach will help you identify a compelling 12 Week Goal and then build a focused plan to reach it. Once your plan is in place, your coach will work with you hand-in-hand to help you execute. We have coaching packages to meet any budget.

TRAIN-THE-TRAINER

The 12 Week Year Train The Trainer (TTT) is a three-day intensive that provides leaders and trainers with everything they need to effectively deliver 12 Week Year training to their teams, and to ensure the long-term uptake of the system.

ACHIEVE! POWER PACK

Everything You Need To Build, Manage & Maintain Your 12 Week Year System. The Achieve Power-Pack is your step-by-step blueprint for plugging into the power of 12 Week Year and achieving more in 12 weeks than most will in 12 months.

ADDITIONAL RESOURCES

12weekyear.com is the home for everything 12 Week Year from 12 Week Year journals, affinity wear, and more!

To learn more contact us at **Support@12weekyear.com**, or call our office at **517.699.3570**

attend Q+A

3 books week 8

Ads.

market research

£6000 passive income

more books

2 hours run a day

Compute KD1 copies

Build design team

Publish book. wrs. By 1 bby week 4

£ Generate book ideas

Proof read

Published 3 nonfiction books un £6000 passive income

Look at budget.

marketing.

Food plan.

lose 28lbs

Find designer & writer.

Olympic triathlon

+ stretch. sharp trans

London 3 time week

Once every day Stretch

Create training plan.

2x bike
2x run
2x swim